LONDON TERMINI
PAST AND PROPOSED

Vic Mitchell

RADIAL RAIL

2003

MP Middleton Press

Cover pictures:
Upper: BR 2-6-4T no. 80018 waits in the terminal part of London Bridge station ready to depart for
Tunbridge Wells West on 4th April 1959. The Thameslink 2000 plan envisages destruction of everything
to the right of the train, but RADIAL RAIL would be the structure's saviour. (J.H.Aston)
Lower: Computer simulation allows a class 319 EMU to pass over Waterloo Road on a bridge not
used by regular passenger trains for more than a century. This link is a key part of RADIAL RAIL
and the scheme for major improvements for London's travellers. (V.Mitchell)

FOREWORD BY Mr. CHRIS GREEN

Managing Director
Network SouthEast 1986-92

Any journey, which includes crossing the centre of London, involves at least one change of train with the honourable exception of Thameslink. Dr Mitchell has identified a number of journeys, which, with a minimum of new railway could be converted to through transits to eliminate wasting changes of train.

But he has gone beyond this basic planning function. Taking today's service patterns as his starting point, he has developed a family of new services, which will exploit to the full the new links, which he is proposing. These not only offer some interesting new journey opportunities such as Surbiton to Hayes via Waterloo, Cannon Street and London Bridge. They will also provide relief to some existing links, which are currently very overcrowded such as the Waterloo and City line.

Implementing his proposals would however conflict with some other schemes currently being promoted. In particular, they would have a significant impact on the south east limb of the Thameslink 2000 scheme.

However, the two are not totally incompatible and it is for the Strategic Railway Authority and Transport *for* London to jointly find the optimum balance in the interests of the travelling public.

This is a refreshing new look at a very old problem. The author is to be congratulated on his innovative approach.

C E W Green
December 2002

Published March 2003
ISBN 1 904474 00 4
© Dr J.C.V. Mitchell, 2003
Published by Middleton Press
   Easebourne Lane
   Midhurst, West Sussex
   GU29 9AZ
Tel: 01730 813169
Fax: 01730 812601
Email: enquiries@middletonpress.fsnet.co.uk
Printed & bound by Biddles Ltd, Kings Lynn

ESSEX
COUNTY COUNCIL
LIBRARY

PROLOGUE AND ACKNOWLEDGEMENTS
TO LONDON TERMINI PAST AND PROPOSED

This volume contains the text and diagrams of the RADIAL RAIL document submitted to the Association of Train Operating Companies, Cross London Rail Links Ltd, Network Rail, the Secretary of State for Transport, the Strategic Rail Authority and Transport *for* London. My additional comments are contained in the map and photograph captions.

I am particularly grateful to Mr Chris Green for providing an encouraging foreword and my sincere thanks for assistance received goes to Edward Dawes, Reg Hawkes and Dennis Lovatt. Norman Langridge, and David and Susan Salter have kindly checked and improved the text which has been typeset by my wife Barbara. Not only that, but she tolerated my observation of the railway scene in South London during our rush-hour travels for the duration of our six years of engagement in the 1950s.

Vic Mitchell
January 2003

PREFACE
TO RADIAL RAIL

With the recent alterations in the organisation of the railways of Britain, it is thought that the time is right to present a scheme that would provide London's surface travellers with an increase in trains running across this great city without terminating and thus greatly reducing changes. It is intended to bring early relief to the intolerable overcrowding suffered by so many.

Environmental and heritage issues have been carefully considered, as have local residents. The benefits extend from Central London to large areas of the Home Counties.

The study is based on the evolution of the railways of the Metropolis and reference is made to illustrations found in various Middleton Press albums. The publishers intend to reproduce this document in expanded form, with extensive illustrations, for publication as a book under the title of *London Termini - Past and Proposed.*

Dr J C V Mitchell
Mitchell Consultancy
Midhurst
December 2002

CONTENTS

1. INTRODUCTION

RADIAL RAIL offers a relatively low cost means of achieving the proposed Thameslink trains frequency enhancement and at the same time greatly increasing the areas served. The service would be extended to lines both south-east and south-west of London.

The proposal would substantially increase cross-London travel opportunities and would facilitate direct access to the new Eurostar terminal under construction. (Chapter 16)

CROSSLOO forms an important part of the scheme. This involves alterations at Waterloo to create two through platforms and a spacious extension of the existing low level concourse, which would reduce congestion and almost double the retail frontage. (Chapter 3)

The CROSS RIVER TRANSIT scheme for a tramway between South and North London, which has been approved by the Mayor of London, would be enhanced by the implementation of RADIAL RAIL, as the opportunity would arise for CRT2, a second and complementary river crossing, providing an additional route in the central area. (Chapter 5)

CRT3 is described, this being a tramway to link South London with the City. This would also use redundant railway track and would thus be similarly low cost. (Chapter 11)

London Bridge station would require only minor alterations and not the major demolition and reconstruction envisaged in the Thameslink 2000 proposal, this reducing financial requirements by a large factor.

The contentious additional viaduct over Borough High Street and Borough Market would not be required, further reducing capital costs and damage to historic structures.

The third feature of Thameslink 2000 was the construction of a new station on Blackfriars Bridge. There were vociferous objections to this as its roof would ruin the vista of the City when viewed downstream. RADIAL RAIL eliminates this problem as it requires only minor changes to Blackfriars and envisages a new station to serve the South Bank area of Southwark, long devoid of a surface station. (Chapters 12 and 13)

With Thameslink 2000 under threat of financial constraints, RADIAL RAIL is an ideal replacement owing to its low capital requirements and high potential for its speedy implementation to bring early relief to the travelling public suffering overcrowding and unnecessary changes.

2. BACKGROUND

2a. Origins of Thameslink

Thameslink (TL) was created in May 1988 by relaying track in tunnels that had been used by north-south passenger trains from 1867 until World War I and by freight for the subsequent 50 years. New trains were required that could operate on two greatly different voltages and collect power from third rail or overhead wire. The changeover point was, and still is, at Farringdon.

The successful genesis of Thameslink from a 1983 GLC report followed the establishment of Network SouthEast on 10th June 1986. It was the first significant example of enterprise to benefit users of surface railways travelling across London since the mid-Victorian period. (Nothing has come to fruition since, but the establishment of the Strategic Rail Authority is a promising sign).

2b. Thameslink success

Initially just linking Brighton and Bedford with two routes through South London, the service was very popular from the outset. Within the first year, passenger traffic between the newly connected places increased by 300%. Between 1993/4 and 1998/9 there was an increase on the already high figures of 57%. This must be compared with an average of 26% for other London services.

Thameslink was extended to Sevenoaks via Swanley after five months and to Guildford via West Croydon in 1990. However, the trains did not use main lines, were relatively slow and were withdrawn.

The main feature of the current timetable continues to be the fast Brighton-Bedford service. In addition, there are stopping trains between the Sutton/Wimbledon loop and Luton.

2c. Thameslink limitations

Whilst it is widely agreed that the core section of the route through City Thameslink is capable of accommodating 24 trains per hour (tph) in each direction, the maximum number to date has been only eight. This has been considered to be due to the limitations of London Bridge station and the viaduct west thereof, over Borough High Street.

Maximum track occupation east of London Bridge and platform restrictions in the station are such that Thameslink services are almost completely diverted via

Elephant & Castle at peak times. For example, there are no northbound TL trains through London Bridge between 0715 and 0909, Mondays to Fridays.

The Bedford line is currently the only route, but work is in hand to provide a link with tracks radiating from Kings Cross, known as the GN lines (ex-Great Northern Railway).

The Thameslink 2000 plan allows for 10 trains per hour on this route and 14 on the Bedford line (ex-Midland Railway). The latter figure is also the present peak hour number on that route.

2d. Thameslink 2000 proposals

Railtrack applied for a Transport and Works Act Order in 1997 and after negotiations with objectors applied for a Variation Order in 1999. Key features being the partial and asymmetric demolition of the historic glazed train shed at London Bridge and the construction of a second viaduct in the vicinity of Borough High Street and Market. This was to allow an increase in train frequency between London Bridge and the Thameslink route.

A further proposal was the extension of Blackfriars station southwards across the bridge over the River Thames. Provision for passenger access to the South Bank from the extended station was made, this being in the vicinity of the developing tourist area around the Tate Modern.

2e. Thameslink 2000 decision

Whilst accepting, after strong criticism, a less visually intrusive Blackfriars station extension, the Inquiry inspector would not agree to the serious damage proposed to London Bridge station or the demolition and disruption envisaged in the Conservation Areas of Southwark, around Borough Market.

The Inquiry began in June 2000, three years after the proposal was made. The report was not issued until January 2002 and is 37mm thick.

The Strategic Rail Authority has been very critical of the proposals made by Railtrack and the consequent serious and unacceptable delays. However, the latter organisation ceased to exist (technically) on 1st October 2002 and a new approach to the intractable problems can be made.

3. CROSSLOO

Crossloo is the proposed link line across Waterloo station.

3a. Origins

The south western and south eastern lines were connected together as long ago as 1864 when a bridge was built over Waterloo Road to carry a link between the London & South Western Railway and the South Eastern Railway.

When the SER extended westward from its terminus at London Bridge to Charing Cross in 1864, it made provision for a City terminus at Cannon Street. This branch opened in 1866 from a triangular junction with the 1864 line. For many decades, most trains served both termini, reversing at Cannon Street. The service provided the first fast link between the City and West End, predating the underground route by 18 years.

The line across Waterloo station was single track and was used for only a few years by a curious circular service operated by the London & North Western Railway between Euston and London Bridge. Subsequently the bridge was used by pedestrians between the two stations at Waterloo.

3b. Revival

The CROSSLOO project forms an important part of the RADIAL RAIL proposal, as it provides an opportunity for an east-west link across London without the expense of tunnelling. It also gives the potential for a connection between the south west routes and those of the north-south axis.

Through running at Waterloo would greatly increase direct travel opportunities and the range of interchange points available to passengers.

The number of terminating trains would be reduced, with the consequent reduction in rolling stock and manpower wastage.

With the successful implementation of CROSSLOO, the much needed RADIAL RAIL system could be fully implemented and the under-utilised Cannon Street station could become the hub of London's surface railways. The minimisation of the impact of CROSSLOO on Waterloo station is discussed in chapter 7.

4. RADIAL RAIL 2003

4a. Aims

The objective is to create a radiating rail network that will cover all points of the compass. Most routes could centre on Cannon Street, but there would be a multitude of other interchange points with surface and underground railways, together with light rail routes.

4b. Train frequencies

4.b.1 Off Peak 2002

Diagram 4.1 indicates trains per hour in the central area. The routes between the Elephant & Castle and Blackfriars, also between Metropolitan Junction and Charing Cross, have four tracks.

Note that the West Spur to Cannon Street shows zero. This has carried no passengers for over 50 years, only empty trains at peak times and is thus a serious waste of resources.

The Moorgate line also indicates zero, as it is only used in peak hours and was listed for closure in the Thameslink 2000 plans.

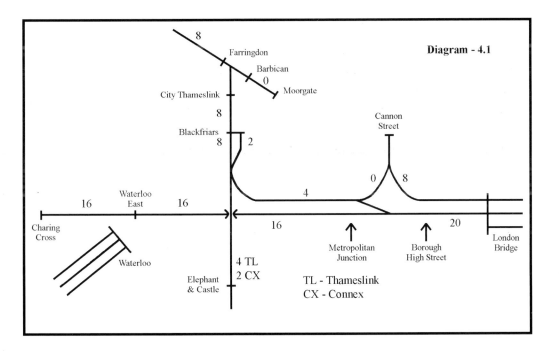

4.b.2 Peak 2002

The most serious operational problem since the inception of Thameslink services in 1988 has been the bottleneck at Borough High Street, where the quadruple tracks from Charing Cross are reduced to two on the viaduct. Thus only one train is shown from London Bridge and Blackfriars. This figure applies from 16.45 to 17.45 for example.

Of the 16 trains passing through Elephant & Castle, six terminate at Blackfriars and two at City Thameslink. Thameslink 2000 envisages the 14tph north of Farringdon being increased to 24.

Note that West Spur carries not a single passenger at any time.

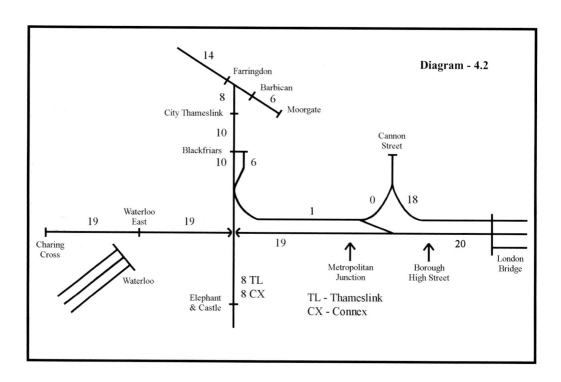

Diagram - 4.2

4.b.3 Peak Targets

The CROSSLOO link is shown with 12tph, this reducing the number serving Charing Cross. Many passengers using that station are changing to or from the Bakerloo or Northern lines, which they could do equally well at Waterloo. The advent of CROSS RIVER TRANSIT 2 trams on a parallel route would provide additional capacity and also an opportunity to change at Waterloo when travelling to many locations north of Charing Cross.

Of the 12 CROSSLOO services, eight could run to destinations north of London by reversal at or near Cannon Street. Two could be for SW-SE London trains and two paths could be dedicated to a SE-NW service.

The issue of trains from the South East that presently terminate at Blackfriars is discussed in chapters 12 and 13.

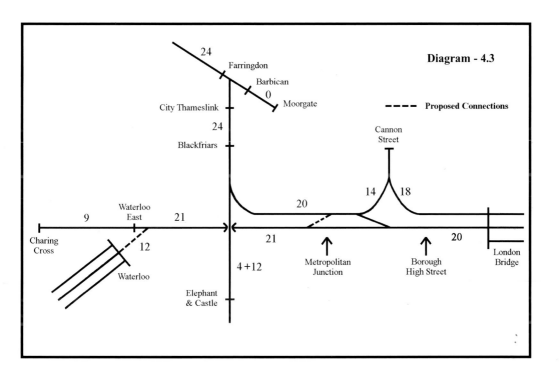

4c. Methodology

4.c.1 List of routes possible through Central London

A   North - South East
B   North - South West
C   North - South Central
       via London Bridge
D   North - South Central
       via Elephant & Castle
E   North West - South East
       via Kensington Olympia
F   Charing Cross - South East
G   Cannon Street - South East
H   South West - South East

Notes

1) Trains terminating at Blackfriars are not shown.
2) North includes those proposed for the north-east via the GN route to Cambridge.
3) C and D represent the present Thameslink routes.
4) B, C and E all reverse at Cannon Street, although B could reverse on West Spur - see chapter 6.
5) The tph figures shown are conjectural and should be based on traffic surveys. They are intended to show the potential of RADIAL RAIL using existing structures.
6) Destination options are considered in chapter 16.

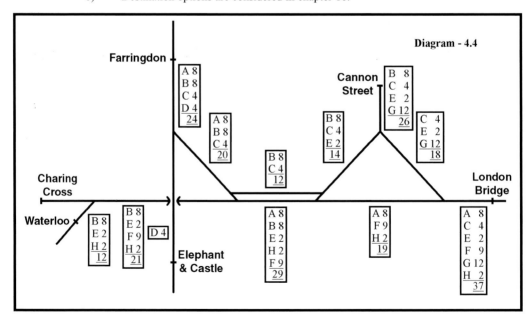

Diagram - 4.4

4.c.2 Track alterations

The items summarised below are considered in more detail in the chapter relating to each location.

a)   Restoration of the link between Waterloo and Waterloo East.
b)   Restoration of the northern track west of Metropolitan Junction.
c)   New crossovers between it and Waterloo East.
d)   Restoration of three tracks on West Curve.
e)   New connections from these into Cannon Street.
f)   Blackfriars Bridge track rearrangement.

Owing to space limitations at all of these sites, grade junctions (i.e. level) are inevitable and thus Synchronised Junction Use (or parallel working) would be essential to maximise their occupation. SJU was practised by skilful signalmen in the days of manual control and can easily be incorporated into the programmes overseen by modern signallers, but its success inevitably depends on train crew availability.

Grade separated junctions (i.e. flyovers and flyunders) are numerous in outer London and additional provisions were identified in the Thameslink 2000 proposal. However, this document does not extend to that topic, as decisions on inner London strategy and train destinations have to be made first. In this context, it is important to recognise that RADIAL RAIL does not increase the train frequency on any route south of the Thames; it redistributes the trains to obtain maximum use of the Thameslink core and also the bridge over Borough High Street without widening, while increasing travel opportunities.

Thus the expensive and destructive schemes of Thameslink 2000 are not required for RADIAL RAIL.

5. CROSS RIVER TRANSIT 2
South London to the West End

5a. The Cross River Partnerships public statement.

What is Cross River Transit?

- It is a scheme being developed by London Transport and the Cross River Partnership, to provide a high quality, surface level, fully accessible public transport link across the heart of London.

- It could use articulated single deck trolley buses (as used in Arnhem, Basel and Zurich) or modern trams as used in Strasbourg, Paris, Manchester and Croydon (from Autumn 1999). The choice of vehicle will depend upon economic and environmental assessments and the result of public consultation.

- Separation from other traffic and priority at traffic signals will ensure that passengers will not be inconvenienced by road congestion.

- The system will be built to the best modern standards. All stops will have shelters, 'real time' information, CCTV, passenger intercom, and access without steps to comfortable, quiet, environmentally friendly vehicles.

- Improved interchanges will allow users to move from buses, trains and Tubes with the minimum of inconvenience.

- The system will be fully integrated in the LT Travelcard system, allowing passengers to hop on and off the system with the minimum of fuss.

What Transit will do for London

Transit is a further step in bringing attractive and accessible surface transport to the heart of the capital. Quick, clean and green, it will contribute towards keeping London a world class city in the 21st century.

Cross River Transit will:

- Provide a real alternative to the private car for trips into and around town;

- Help people get between mainline stations and jobs and entertainment centres;

- Link the busy tourist areas around Covent Garden with a revitalised South Bank;

- Give residents of Camden and Peckham a reliable environmentally friendly and congestion free link to the centre of London;

- Help reduce overcrowding on the inner sections of a number of busy Tube lines;

- Give an opportunity to improve the townscape of a number of important areas, and reduce the space used by cars.

5b. The Proposal

The extent of the approved light rail system is shown with dashes, together with some of the potential stopping places. The proposed additional route (CRT2) has been superimposed with a solid line, it crossing the Thames on Hungerford Bridge. CRT3 is described in chapter 12.

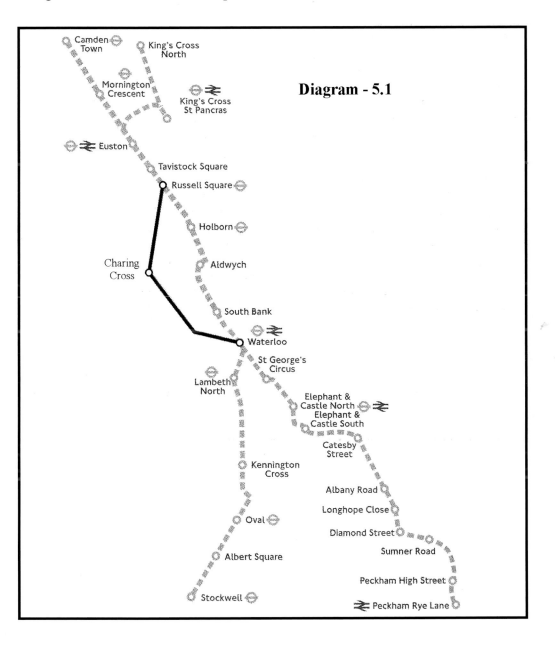

Diagram - 5.1

5c. Benefits

The merits of the approved Cross River Transit are numerous, but a potential limitation results from it having only one core route, which could be subject to overcrowding and delays due to road traffic problems and roadworks.

The proposed additional route in the central area would have the following benefits:

a)   A greater choice of destinations and interchange points for users of Cross River Transit.

b)   An enhanced service over Hungerford Bridge.

c)   Reduced congestion on Waterloo Bridge and in Kingsway.

d)   Improved public transport for Covent Garden, British Museum and London University Senate.

e)   Elimination of the **dangerous overcrowding** at Covent Garden Underground station and its restricting lifts.

f)   Public transport to the centre of Covent Garden.

g)   The option of a short heritage tram circuit, to benefit tourism and enhance London's transport museum. There is no such facility in the South of England.

5d. Methodology

CROSS RIVER TRANSIT 2 would diverge from the approved Cross River Transit in Waterloo Road, near the bridge carrying the present four railway tracks to Charing Cross. As two of these would become redundant with the advent of CROSSLOO, the eastern pair on Hungerford Bridge would carry trams to Charing Cross.

Trams from the south would first pass over York Road on the existing railway bridge. An initial estimate gives a gradient of 1 in 17 up to it from Waterloo Road, well within the operating parameters for modern tramways. The tracks would be close to the existing brick viaduct and rise up onto it at the north end of the incline.

The gradient of the incline would be reduced near its mid-point to allow a stop to be provided close to the existing row of stops for northbound buses, but at a higher level.

At Charing Cross, CROSS RIVER TRANSIT 2 would leave railway property at the north end of Villiers Street. It would impinge upon a small part of two floors adjacent to the north east elevation of the Charing Cross Hotel, but not its facade. This structure appears no longer to be railway property, being a Thistle Hotel. Its occupier at the time of the new work could be given, as part of the intrusion compensation, the opportunity of having a tram stop called "Charing Cross Thistle", for example.

The hotel would thus be able to make a unique claim that it has direct rapid transit access to four national rail terminals and two international ones from its ground floor. A single track tramway would be necessary in this vicinity.

Trams would cross The Strand on the level, the traffic lights synchronising their passage with the pedestrian phase to minimise highway occupation time.

The route northwards to Russell Square is outside the scope of the present work, but the use of single tracks in parallel narrow streets could be considered, as this has proved acceptable in many cities in mainland Europe.

The proposed supplementary tram route could be constructed in two stages, north and south of The Strand, if circumstances prevented an integrated implementation. As each half brings so many benefits, one section should be commissioned on its own if necessary.

The southern half, over the Thames, could even be operational before the main route of Cross River Transit and serve as a proving ground for the trams, free of road traffic.

5.2   Seen in the depot of Croydon Tramlink on 17th June 2001 is one of the six-axle trams built by Bombadier in Vienna. They are similar to those used in Cologne and this type might be seen crossing the Thames on three different bridges in the future. (D.Salter)

6. CANNON STREET

6a. Background

Opening on 1st September 1866, the station mainly served SER routes to Kent and also offered the only trains between the City and the West End for almost 20 years. Many trains between Charing Cross and Kent continued to reverse here until 1916. Electrification began in 1926, the first routes so treated including those to Orpington and Hayes. As others followed, the reversals diminished and eventually ceased altogether.

The final platform to receive a conductor rail was no. 8. This was in 1959, when Kent Coast services were electrified. Most platforms had been extended to accommodate the 10 coaches of the North Kent trains by 1957. Further extensions took place in 1991 for the Networker 12-car trains, but there were only seven platforms subsequently.

6b. Services in 2002

There are eight departures per hour from 0611 to 2018, Mondays to Fridays, and from 0829 to 1859 on Saturdays. These are mostly destined for Dartford by different routes, but there is an hourly service to Ashford via Maidstone West. There are no trains on Sundays.

The evening peak hour (1700 to 1800) has 12 suburban departures, plus six for the main lines. Empty stock for some of these services is kept south of the station, while other sets stand in sidings south of Blackfriars Bridge.

The station has seven platforms and all are accessible from the east, but only numbers 4 to 7 can be reached from the west at present. All platforms accept 12 coach trains.

6c. RADIAL RAIL

Once again, Cannon Street would be regarded as a through station, with only some peak time trains terminating. With a second driver ready to take the train on, dwell times need be little more than at other principal stations.

The southern part of the City of London would benefit from a direct rail link with a greatly increased number of stations, on all points of the compass potentially.

This increased choice of destinations would reduce the number of passengers changing (and delaying) trains elsewhere, not only at London Bridge but also at

Waterloo. Through running from this station would also reduce the heavy loading of the Waterloo & City underground line at peak times.

6d. Route options

    B   North - South West
            (via Waterloo)
    C   North - South Central
            (the present Thameslink)
    E   North West - South East
            (via Kensington Olympia and Waterloo)

The route diagram is in paragraph 4.c.1 and the potential destinations are listed in chapter 16.

Reference: Pictures 1 to 6 in *Charing Cross to Dartford* and 1 to 8 in *Charing Cross to Orpington*.

6.1   This engraving depicts the station about ten years after its opening and includes the two public footpaths for which users paid a toll. There were only five tracks on the bridge until 1893, after which time the number was doubled. (Pamlin Prints)

6.2   The upper four floors served as a hotel, but lacking continental traffic it was not a great success and so the bedrooms became railway offices in 1931. The main rooms were retained for functions until World War II. (Lens of Sutton)

6.3   The southern end of the station was recorded on a postcard and it features the second signal box, which was in use from 1893 until 1926. It had an amazing 243 levers. (Lens of Sutton)

6.4 A photograph from 12th April 1958 reveals that there were connections from West Curve to all the platforms at that time. The tower on the right contained a water tank, which supplied the locomotives and other requirements. (A.E.Bennett)

6.5 A more distant view from the same period includes the monument to the 1666 Fire of London in the right background. Hawkshaw's roof was supported on 27 million bricks, but all its glass was lost during the Nazi bombing raids. (Lens of Sutton)

*6.6   No. 30925 **Cheltenham** was a 4-4-0 of the "Schools" class and is seen at the head of a Hastings train shortly before all such trains were operated by diesel electric units of the type shown in picture no. 8.3. The changeover was in 1958. Note the recently extended platforms. (A.E.Bennett)*

6.7   This is the view from the cab road shortly before the gates and trellis barriers were removed to allow completion of platform lengthening. The framework had supported temporary roofing since WWII. (Lens of Sutton)

6.8   The other end of the temporary canopy over platforms 5 and 6 is seen not long before its demolition. The weather protection over platforms 1-4 was even shorter; the scrap train has arrived. (Lens of Sutton)

6.9   Viewed from a special train on 18th April 1960, the station was in transition and one could see through the remaining bedroom windows. More than 1000 tons of steel had been removed, the enemy having dealt with almost two acres of glass. (A.E.Bennett)

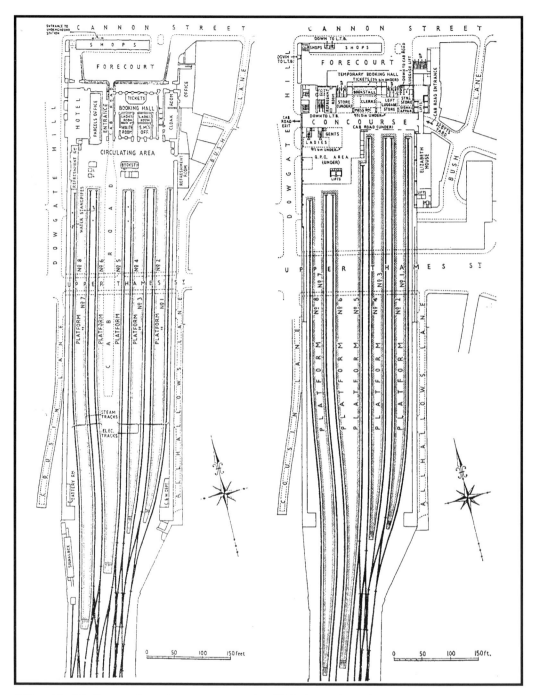

6.10   The left diagram shows the arrangement after 1926 when only platforms 1 to 5 were electrified. The plan on the right is from 1964 and includes the then recently widened Upper Thames Street under the platforms and includes evidence that the GPO (Royal Mail) was by then under the concourse. (Railway Magazine)

6.11 Massive office developments above the station started in 1988, the structure requiring 9500 tons of steel. The resulting bland street frontage is seen on 9th November 2002; the Underground station is closed on Saturdays and Sundays. (V.Mitchell)

6.12 The south end is seen on the same day, with part of the six-storey block evident. Artificial lighting has been required since 1991, but at least the weather protection has improved greatly. The old platform 1 was eliminated at that time. (V.Mitchell)

7. WATERLOO

7a. Background

The LSWR terminus opened in 1848 and was extended in stages, to become effectively three separate stations. The link across Waterloo Road to the SER was added between two of the original three platforms in 1864.

Rebuilding of the terminus into its present form was started in 1903, but it was not completed until 1922, due to the complexity of the task and the intervention of World War I.

The link line over Waterloo Road was lifted in 1911, but its bridge remains in place today, although a cab road and offices were built across its route.

The 21 platforms remained little altered until 2nd July 1990 when platforms 12-15 were renumbered 14 to 17 and two new platforms came into use. The space was made by reducing the width of the central cab road. This was in readiness for the creation of a new station for international services. This opened on 14th November 1994, the platforms being numbered 20 to 24.

7b. Services in 2002

Unlike the other termini serving the South, the basic route pattern radiates fan like, although some form loops which centre on Hounslow and Kingston.

Beyond the station approach, there are eight parallel tracks, only the northern one being signalled for reversible running. It is used mainly for Eurostar services. There are three berthing sidings, these being for suburban stock.

Platforms 1 to 6 accommodate 8 cars, while 7 to 19 mostly take 12. Long distance trains are centred on 7 to 16, while those running via Barnes (the "Windsor" lines) use the higher numbers. Platforms 20-24 comprise the separate Eurostar section, known as "Waterloo International".

7c. RADIAL RAIL

Here we consider the CROSSLOO proposal in more detail and, most importantly, its impact on the concourse. This was successfully altered in the early 1990s, when a low level concourse was created for the international platforms.

Much of Waterloo was constructed by building two layers of brick arches, one on top of the other, thus the station is at third floor level. To accommodate CROSSLOO easily, a southward extension of the low level concourse is proposed.

The edges of the high level one would be retained as walkways, in a manner that has been successfully achieved at Liverpool Street station.

Thus a circulating area would be created between platforms 24 and 7, with the CROSSLOO tracks passing overhead, probably on existing arches. If at the wrong level, their abutments might carry new I beams or concrete slabs cast in situ.

7d. Low Level Concourse

The advantage of a low level concourse:
  i) Easier access from most underground platforms.
  ii) Easier access from Waterloo Road.
  iii) Easier access to Waterloo Road northbound bus stops.
  iv) Easy access to the north side cab rank.
  v) The potential to lengthen platforms 1 to 6 for 12 cars.
  vi) Retail frontage would be more than doubled.
  vii) The fine curved facade of the Edwardian railway office block would be retained and the net impact of CROSSRAIL on it would be zero.
  viii) The undesirable effect on the ambiance of the station of the recent modular offices raised on ugly stilts over the platforms would be lessened by having a lower eye level from most viewpoints.
  ix) At present cabs discharge their users in the rain at the south entrance and then wait in the dry under the roof at the east end of the station. As the cab road would be blocked by CROSSLOO, taxis would load and turn under this roof and depart on the road on which they had arrived. Many do this already.
  x) Cab road buses would need new stopping places; these would be near Victory Arch. This would give better access from the low level concourse, particularly for the mobility impaired. Buses would arrive from and depart to York Road.
  xi) The provision of walkways each side of glazed panels parallel to the CROSSLOO tracks would link the flanks of the upper concourse. These would be parallel to the platform barriers and to the existing retail outlets in the lower floor of the office block.
  xii) Total concourse floor area is increased allowing better crowd dispersal at times of delay. This would be aided by more departure displays, with larger lettering. The low level concourse would be larger than the shaded area, as it would extend below the upper one, which would thus become a partial gallery.

xiii) The operation of through trains would reduce the number of people using the concourses and thus congestion at peak times.

7e. Route options

B   North - South West
E   North West - South East
H   South West - South East

The route diagram is in paragraph 4.c.1 and the potential destinations are listed in chapter 16.

Reference: Pictures 1 to 20 in *Waterloo to Woking* and 1 to 13 in *Waterloo to Windsor*.

—————————▶

Diagram 7.1. There is a cab road each side of Central Station from the centre track of which is the 1864 link to the SER. On the south side of the link track is a platform which predates platforms A to D. The centre of the three tracks was initially used by trains shuttling between Charing Cross and Cannon Street. The subway shown was later replaced by a footbridge, probably in 1901, when a fourth track was added, south of the others. The map is from 1895.

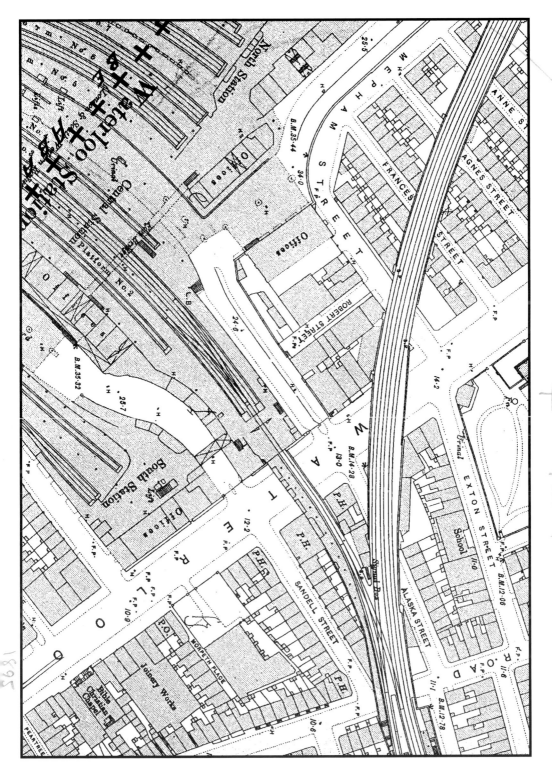

not sure 4 or 6 drks

?

1/2500 ?

N

1895

Diagram 7.2   A plan drawn in 1998 was still relevant in 2002, except that it does not include the subsequent passage and escalators providing access between the concourse and northbound bus stops in Tenison Way. The shaded area represents the low level concourse used by international passengers.

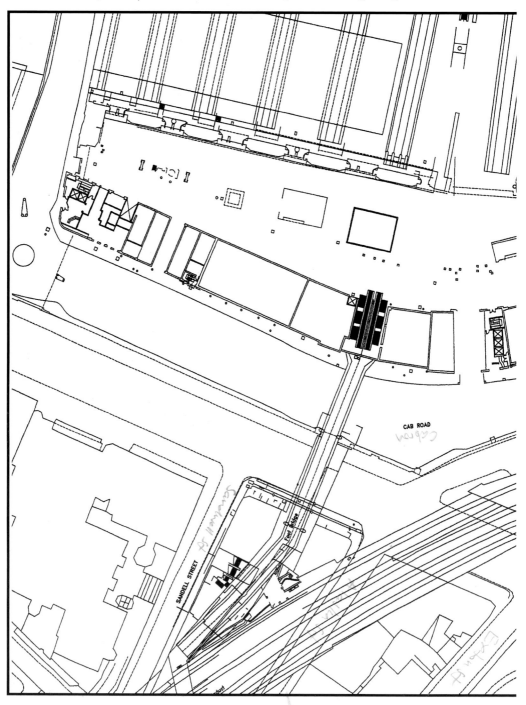

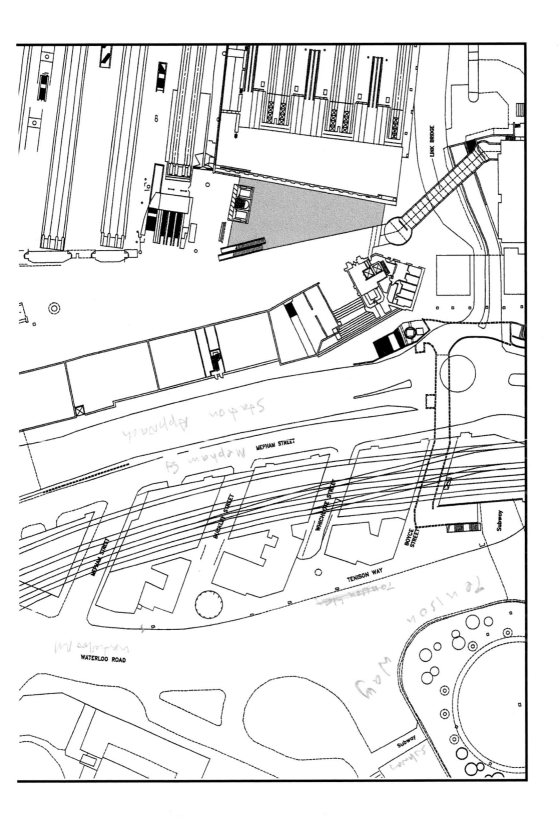

LINK BRIDGE

Stadion Approach

MEPHAM STREET

Mepham St

MEPHAM STREET

BUCKLEY STREET

WINCHCOMBE STREET

BOYCE STREET

Subway

TENISON WAY

Tenison St

WATERLOO ROAD

Tenison Way

Subway

Comyn St

upside down
no scale — no north pan

*Diagram 7.3 The same plan has the proposed low level concourse extension shaded, it passing under the two **CROSSLOO** lines, which are shown with dashes, in their approximate positions. One arises directly from platform 11, while the other would require some realignment of platform 12.*

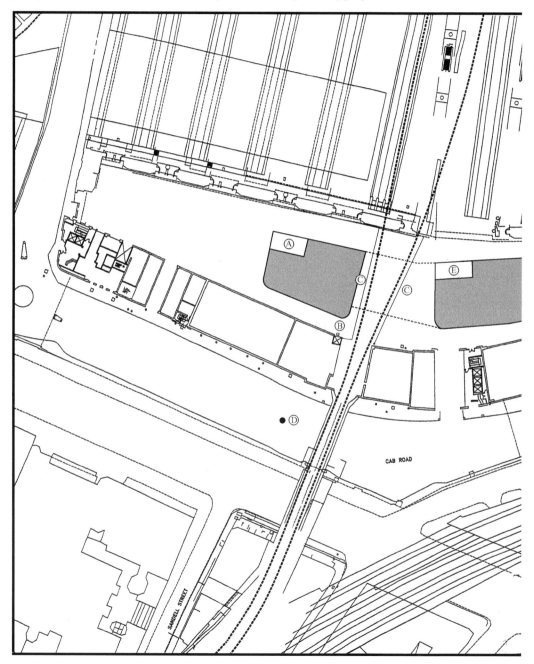

A   Position of existing stairs to the Underground. These would be supplemented by two escalators to the low level concourse, from where Jubilee Line access is at present.
B   Existing lift would be lowered to link two concourse levels.
C   Walkways over lower concourse, flanked by glass panels to retain the present vista.
D   Turning point for cabs at the existing mini-roundabout.
E   Location of two new escalators between high and low level concourses.

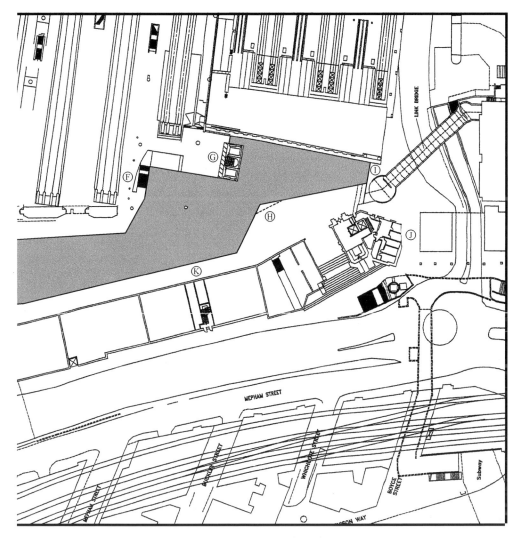

F   The southern two escalators would be retained to serve platforms 12 to 19. The others would be shortened to end at the low level concourse, along with the one existing.
G   The two present lifts would remain, although only one seems necessary.
H   The Eurostar booking hall glass wall would require slight repositioning, to reduce the pinch point. Eurostar marketing would benefit from increased exposure here.
I   Existing doors provide access to the cab rank and the main approach road.
J   The lower floor of the main building would require minor alterations to create a parallel passage, suitable for the main pedestrian entrance from the north. The Victory Arch would still be used by those using platforms 12 to 19.
K   Existing escalator for northbound bus users would be supplemented by a passage from the low level concourse.

7.4   By 1900, there were platforms of assorted widths and very various lengths both sides of the original ones, which are right of centre. Rebuilding was long overdue. The original link line crossed the concourse on the level and is illustrated in **Waterloo to Woking.** *(Lens of Sutton)*

7.5   This signal box had 266 levers, many performing multiple functions. It was in use from 1892 until 1936, but was photographed prior to 1902 when the Necropolis station (right) was demolished. This was used exclusively by funeral trains bound for Brookwood; a replacement was built further south. (Lens of Sutton)

7.6   Two postcard views show the station in metamorphosis in the early years of the 20th century. Parts of the old South Station are still to be seen, but there are no conductor rails. These appeared in 1915-16. (Lens of Sutton)

7.7   The ruin on the right is probably part of the original station. W.H.Smith's premises are arranged tidily on the flank of the concourse, instead of obstructing the centre of it, as at present. The proposed new concourse would present an opportunity to rectify this intrusion. (Lens of Sutton)

7.8   The Waterloo & City Railway's platforms of 1898 are included to emphasise the fact that the main station is composed of brick arches upon brick arches. These platforms are at 90 degrees to those above. (Lens of Sutton)

7.9   This panorama is probably from the 1920s and includes the glazed end of the new roof. The main line platforms did not receive conductor rails until the 1930s. (Lens of Sutton)

7.10   The Victory Arch is above the taxi in this view from June 1953 when the station was decorated for the celebration of the coronation. The line to Charing Cross is high up, on the left. (D.Cullum)

7.11   Seen on the same day is the cab road between platforms 11 and 12, which were often used by the Southampton boat trains. Taxis arrived via a ramp up from Westminster Bridge Road. The white vehicles are LCC Daimler ambulances. (D.Cullum)

7.12   The headcode 80 indicated Portsmouth Harbour, a route that was electrified in 1937. This brought conductor rails to the central part of Waterloo. Standing on the left on 14th March 1967 is no. 34004 Yeovil *with the 13.30 to Weymouth. Steam would vanish within a few weeks on regular services south of the Thames. (J.Scrace)*

7.13   The previous photograph was taken from near the white hut in the centre of this August 1967 panorama. On the right is the flat roof of the 1936 signal box. (C.F.B.Penley/A.C.Mott)

7.14 This eastward view has the exit for cabs on the right and was taken in 1969 from the relatively new footbridge erected across York Road to link the station with the Shell Centre. The proposed platforms 25 and 26 would be to the right of the bridge. (D.Cullum)

7.15 The 1936 signal box had 309 miniature levers and had to be demolished soon after this photograph was taken in October 1989, in order to make way for international trains. A temporary panel was used on the opposite side of the tracks prior to transfer of control to Wimbledon. (V.Mitchell)

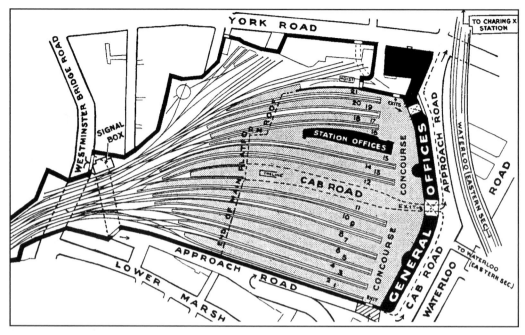

7.16   The 1948 plan was largely still unaltered when work started on rebuilding the north side in 1990. "Hoist" refers to the lift for Waterloo & City line coaches, some of which can be seen in the background of photo 7.15. (Railway Magazine)

7.17   Two photographs from June 1991 show that the "Windsor" platforms (16-21) were removed, together with the short sidings north thereof. The two new platforms for local trains are on the left. (V.Mitchell)

7.18   The top layer of arches that were once under platform 16 are evident as work proceeds on creating Britain's first international terminal, excluding the "Night Ferry" platform at Victoria, long served by direct trains to and from Paris and Brussels. (V.Mitchell)

7.19   Many of the roof spans were in place when the new very long platform 19 was photographed on 21st February 1992. This was outside the international station and was used by the Penzance sleeping car trains from May 1995 until September 1998. (V.Mitchell)

7.20   We finish our survey of this widely admired station with four photographs from 9th November 2002. This features "Wessex" EMUs either side of the new canopy on platforms 13/14, while cones on 11/12 protect the stumps awaiting a new superstructure that should protect future passengers for Cannon Street. (V.Mitchell)

7.21   The white area near the taxi is marked D on diagram 7.3 and it allows vehicles to turn here. Above the three parked cars is the pedestrian bridge linking platforms A to D to the concourse escalators, shown on diagram 7.2. These came into use in Janury 1993 and would all be removed to allow the CROSSLOO plan to be implemented for RADIAL RAIL. (V.Mitchell)

7.22   A view in the other direction shows the northern part of the cab road that would have a similar turning circle north of the CROSSLOO tracks. A subway exists under this road and would provide access to the proposed platforms 25 and 26, which would be upper right. (V.Mitchell)

7.23   A northward view of Waterloo Road has the 1864 rail link bridge above the bus. It was used by passengers on foot until 1993, since when they have been confined to the tube above it. Compare this with the lower cover picture. (V.Mitchell)

8. WATERLOO EAST

8a.   Background

The station opened in 1869, five years after LNWR trains had commenced running between Waterloo and Cannon Street. The platforms had to be built east of the junction and were thus appropriately named "Waterloo Junction". The remoteness of these platforms from the main station has been a disadvantage ever since.

The station was renamed "Waterloo Eastern" in 1935 and "Waterloo East" in 1977, but no attempts seem to have been made to move it westward and passengers have had to suffer the inconvenience of its distant location for generations.

To avoid confusion with the platforms at the main station, those here were (and are) designated A, B, C and D, from north to south.

8b.   Services in 2002

Please see section 9b, under Charing Cross, as all trains call at Waterloo East. Suburban down services mostly use platform A, while longer distance trains stop at platform C.

8c.   RADIAL RAIL

The 12 CROSSLOO trains per hour would use the tracks through platforms C and D, which would be closed as trains would stop at platforms 11 and 12 instead, the lines having been diverted over Waterloo Road.

The tracks through platforms A and B would be slewed west thereof, so that the remaining nine trains per hour to Charing Cross would run on the west side of Hungerford Bridge. These platforms would also be closed, to be replaced by new ones further west, as part of a new interchange between York Road and Waterloo Road.

The platforms would be numbered 25 and 26, owing to their proximity to 24. Access would be from the archway through which passengers currently pass from the concourse to the northbound bus stops. The existing escalator would be largely redundant, as most passengers would walk direct from the low level concourse.

The archway would also pass below the proposed CRT2 tramway and give access to its platforms. A stop would be provided here on the incline mentioned in 5d. An island platform would have access to the subway and its faces could be numbered 27 and 28.

Thus an efficient new interchange between the new concourse, trams, buses and Kent trains would be created and the bad features of Waterloo East lost for ever. Its east end is so remote that it has justified a separate station on the Jubilee Line. This is named Southwark and would continue to serve travellers in that area.

The complex bridge structures in this vicinity might preclude parts of this proposal. An alternative scheme has been prepared for a fresh access to platforms A and B.

8d. Route options

B   North - South West
E   North West - South East
H   South West - South East

These are in addition to the Kent services chosen to continue to use Charing Cross.

The route diagram is in paragraph 4.c.1 and the potential destinations are listed in chapter 16.

Reference: Pictures 10 to 13 in *Charing Cross to Dartford* and 10 to 12 in *Charing Cross to Orpington*.

8.1   A 1962 panorama from the back of the general offices has platforms A to D in the centre with the link span over Waterloo Road lower right. The single track flanked by lattice girders was added in 1901. (J.Scrace)

8.2   In the background is the rear of the general offices and in the centre is the platform used by through trains between 1864 and 1869. The canopy also appears in the previous picture and it sheltered passengers taking the unwanted (and unnecessary) long walk between the stations until 1986, when shops were built on the bridge. (Lens of Sutton)

8.3   Calling at platforms C and D regularly from 1958 until 1986 were diesel-electric units with special narrow bodies designed to suit the restricted tunnels between Tonbridge and Hastings. (D.Cullum)

8.4   Trains terminated at platforms A and B during the reconstruction of Hungerford Bridge in 1979-80 and the distant scissors crossover was provided for this purpose. The bridge in the background carries trains between Blackfriars and Elephant & Castle. (D.Clayton)

8.5   A temporary additional footbridge was provided from which this (and the previous picture) was taken. Passengers from platform D cross the tracks twice on their long hike to the main station, visible beyond the footbridge.

8.6   *A closer view of the bridge just mentioned (but in 1995) includes CCTV for driver-only operation of suburban trains. This train from the Kent Coast is passing under the second footbridge. All would be removed with the advent of RADIAL RAIL. (V.Mitchell)*

8.7   *A view towards Charing Cross from the last mentioned bridge in 2002 shows the area in which platforms 25 and 26 would be provided, after the tracks had been reduced to one pair and repositioned. Some alteration of the steelwork would be required. (V.Mitchell)*

9. CHARING CROSS

9a. Background

The station was built on the site of Mr. Hungerford's market. Mr. I.K.Brunel's suspension bridge from it to Lambeth was dismantled to make way for the 1864 railway bridge. The station's glazed arched roof partially collapsed in 1905 and was replaced by a lattice girder structure, which gave a pleasant light and airy ambience over the six platforms. This was lost in 1988 by the imposition of an office block over them.

9b. Services in 2002

The basic weekday service each hour comprises two trains to Hayes, Hastings, Tunbridge Wells, Gravesend, Dartford and Gillingham, with one to Margate, Dover, Sevenoaks and Orpington. This total of 16 is exceeded by only three between 1700 and 1800, these not stopping at London Bridge.

9c. RADIAL RAIL

The station does not feature in the proposed radiating network, but would be retained with a train every 4 minutes or less to Waterloo and London Bridge, these serving much of Kent as at present.

Some passengers would lose direct travel opportunities to and from Charing Cross, but many more would gain them or better interchange options with the development of RADIAL RAIL.

Those arriving here from the north by Bakerloo or Northern lines could equally well join those services transferred to RADIAL RAIL at Waterloo. Others could use the proposed CRT2 (chapter 5) from areas north of the station to reach Waterloo.

Reference: Pictures 1 to 7 in *Charing Cross to Dartford* and 1 to 8 in *Charing Cross to Orpington*.

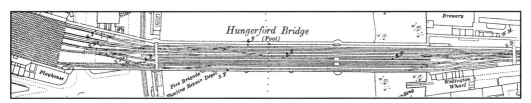

9.1   The 1916 map has the four runnng lines increasing to seven on the bridge and two signal boxes spanning them.

9.2   The Charing Cross Hotel was built over the entrances and a replica of the Eleanor Cross was made for the forecourt. The hotel was used by continental travellers until 1920, when all such services were centred on Victoria. (Lens of Sutton)

9.3   The replacement roof is seen bearing the South Eastern & Chatham Railway's initials. These were changed to SR after the formation of the Southern Railway in 1923. No. 165 is one of the E class 4-4-0s introduced in 1919-20 by the SECR. (National Railway Museum)

9.4   An April 1967 panorama from the Shell Centre reveals that the bridge structure allows for two, one and four tracks. The aerial signal box was in use until 1976, when a panel at London Bridge took over the colour light signals that were installed in 1926. (C.F.B.Penley/A.C.Mott)

9.5   This is a 1969 close-up of the train seen on the bridge. The experimental eight-coach train was built in 1949, but no more followed owing to the long stations stops it required. Platform lengthening was eventually embarked upon. (E.Wilmshurst)

9.6   *EPB units were to be seen under the crest for about 40 years. Work began in 1988 to hang a nine-storey office complex from bowstring structures. These can be seen in the background of picture 7.22. A new durable crest was provided, but permanent platform lighting was needed thereafter. (Lens of Sutton)*

9.7   *This is Villiers Street, which can be seen left of centre in picture 9.4. It is now pedestrianised and would have to accommodate a single tram track, which would emerge from the side of the hotel in about the centre of the picture. One of the Bakerloo line entrances is in the foreground. (V.Mitchell)*

10. METROPOLITAN JUNCTION

10a. Background

The London Chatham & Dover Railway's branch to the City (Blackfriars) via Elephant & Castle was known as the "Metropolitan Extension". A link between it and the SER opened in 1878 and the connection with the latter was thus named "Metropolitan Junction".

It carried an intensive service between North and South East London, links being provided between such places as Finsbury Park and Woolwich Arsenal. Through services were withdrawn in 1917, as the route was required for the mass movement of men and munitions for World War I.

For various reasons, including apathy, regular freight trains and lack of a Strategic Rail Authority, through running was not resumed for passengers. One nocturnal train was the exception for many years. Cross London goods trains ceased in 1969 and apathy prevailed until 1988, when Network SouthEast introduced Thameslink.

10b. Services in 2002

The link has been used by four trains per hour, running between Bedford and Brighton. The junction is also used by some 20 trains per hour from Charing Cross, but no station has been provided in this area, except for a period in the 1860s.

10c. RADIAL RAIL

The junction is a critical location in the proposal, as it limits the number of conflicting movements. It can be regarded as the crossroads of the system and would require a special strategy.

Currently the Blackfriars - Cannon Street link reduces to one track in this vicinity, but could be doubled again. Three tracks could easily be replaced on West Spur; the reduction to five tracks through the junction area would require critical traffic management over a short distance.

The operational and reliability benefits to be achieved by providing three tracks on West Spur are numerous. This would be one of the most heavily used sections of the system and thus trains could be recessed here at times of congestion or awaiting a platform vacancy at Cannon Street. There are a complementary three tracks on East Curve at present.

The diagram in para 4.c.1 shows eight trains per hour (B8) available North-South West, but operationally it would mean 16 trains in that direction using West Spur, due to reversals. Thus provision would be required for trains to be reversed on any one of the three lines. This flexibility would be advantageous at peak times and could be timetabled accordingly or, in emergencies, could be implemented by PA announcements. Cannon Street is currently closed on Sundays and late evenings and could thus remain so. At such times, the driver could simply walk through the train. At busy times, a relief driver would be ready to take the train away in the opposite direction. Short staff platforms with shelters and suitable walkways would be required on West Curve.

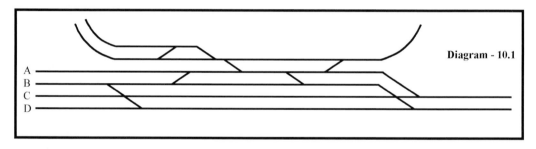

Diagram 10.1 Lower right on the current diagram is the double track over Borough Market which forms the bottleneck for services on the Charing Cross quadruple track. The Cannon Street single track (West Curve) is used by empty stock only. On the left of both diagrams are the relevant Waterloo platforms numbers.

Diagram 10.2 The diagram shows all passenger tracks relaid to their previous optimum, albeit with connections revised. The dashes indicate track required.

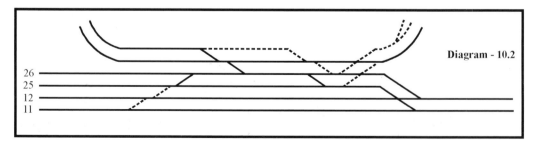

10.3   A westward view from 1991 has the four Charing Cross lines on the left and the short section of single track for trains to and from Blackfriars in the right middle distance. This would be doubled again. (V.Mitchell)

10.4   Looking in the other direction from a train running from London Bridge to Waterloo East, we see empty stock running on the West Curve to Cannon Street. This would have three tracks again and earn revenue, large amounts of it. (V.Mitchell)

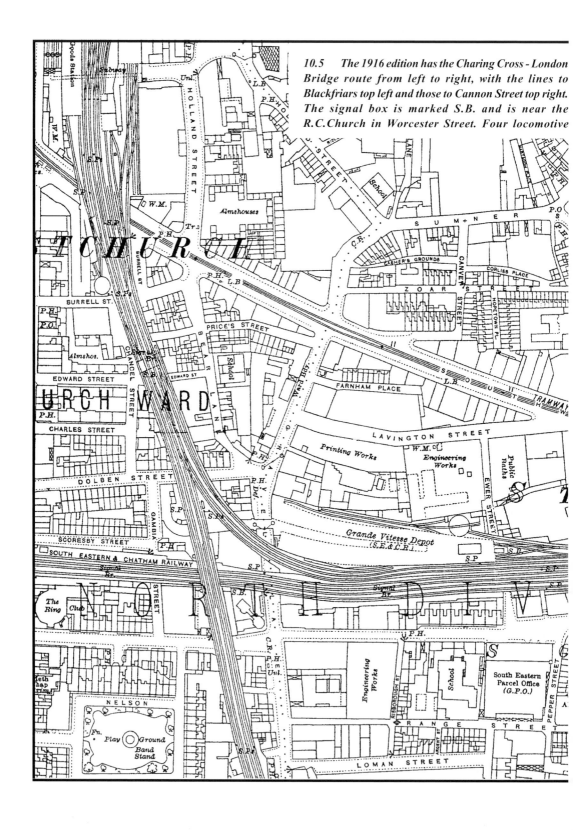

*urntables are also featured, as are numerous street
ramways. These are illustrated in the albums listed on
he final page of this volume. The addition of a sixth
rack east of the junction would increase capacity greatly
nd would require the purchase of very little land.*

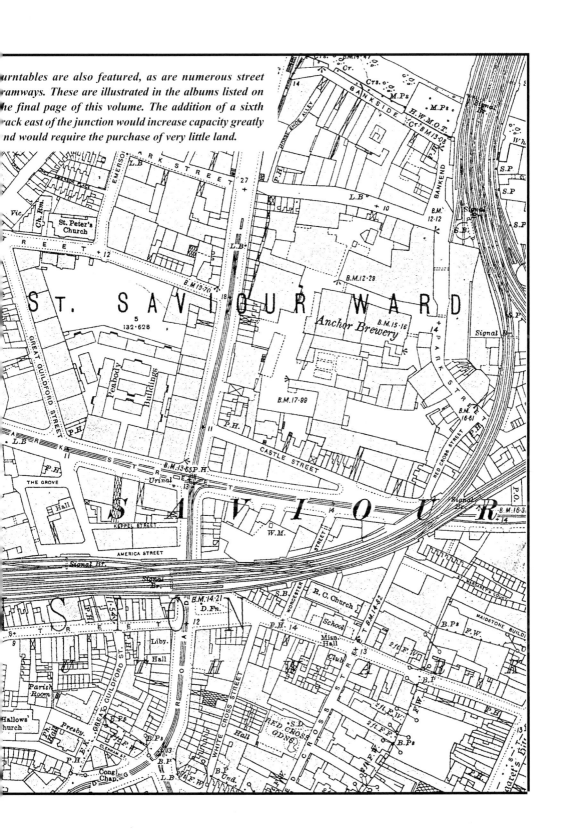

11. CROSS RIVER TRANSIT 3
South London to the City

11a. The proposal

The light rail route would run parallel to Walworth and Camberwell Roads, thus reducing traffic thereon. It would serve the area between the two approved CRT routes and both would have the advantage of connections at Elephant & Castle with the route running close to Blackfriars Road to the City.

CRT3 would use the eastern pair of existing tracks north of Loughborough Junction to Blackfriars. Its terminus there would have to be north of the station, to avoid conflict with heavy rail services running via Denmark Hill. The western pair would be below their maximum capacity with the proposed 16tph on the route.

Only one new structure would be required and this is a flyover to carry the trams above the curve used by Blackfriars - Metropolitan Junction trains. Its southern end would be on the bridge carrying trains over the Charing Cross - Metropolitan Junction line.

A connection near Elephant & Castle would be required for stock movements, if the efficiency of having a single depot were to be realised.

Thus civil engineering work would involve only one flyover and the northern terminus would be the existing terminal platforms at Blackfriars station, much shortened.

A 3.3 mile long light rail modern transport corridor would thus be created using existing track and having no highway impact.

11b Benefits

a) Enhanced speedy transport between South London and the City.
b) Reduced demand on the often overcrowded north-south buses.
c) Potential extension through the streets to Brixton, if overhead electrification was employed.
d) Potential extension underground to Bank, to connect with the Docklands Light Railway, if inverted conductor rails were used.

Diagram 11.1   The approved Cross River Transit is shown with dashes, along with the proposed stops. CRT3 is marked with a solid line, plus the proposed new station and two that were closed in 1916. Other stops would be likely, including one at Borough Road, where there was a station until 1908.

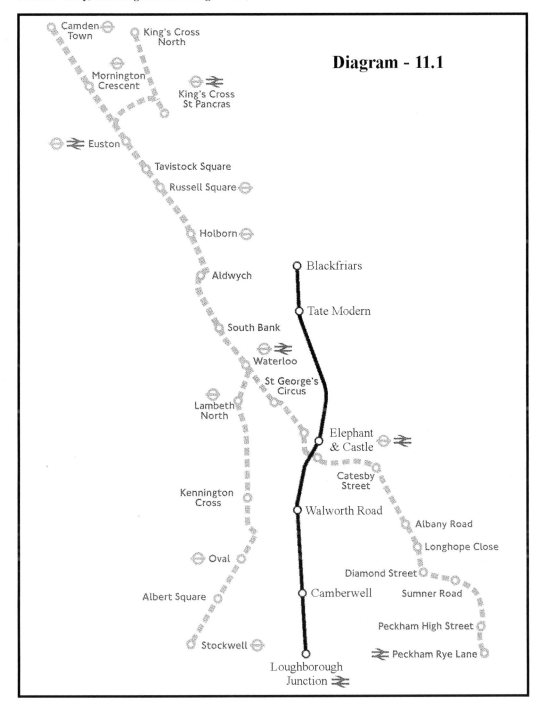

Diagram - 11.1

11.2   *This sequence of photographs take us on a journey south from Elephant & Castle to Loughborough Junction. This is Elephant & Castle in 1990. CRT3 trams would use the tracks and platforms on the left. The other lines were once roofed over here. (J.Scrace)*

11.3   *Walworth Coal Sidings were north of Walworth station and were designed so that wagons could be emptied under the roof. The coal was sent down chutes to stores under the arches. The goods train is destined for North London (Ferme Park) on 1st March 1957 and includes two cattle wagons at the front. (R.C.Riley/Transport Treasury)*

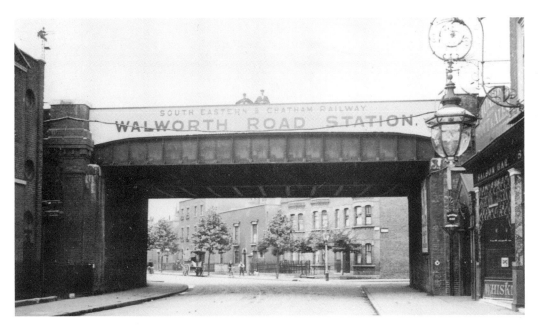

11.4   The station was opened as Camberwell Gate in 1863 and renamed in 1865. Platforms were only provided on the western pair of tracks and they were closed on 3rd April 1916, when the Moorgate service was withdrawn. (Lens of Sutton)

11.5   Loughborough Junction is a railway crossroads with spurs between the north, east and west routes. All are still in use and dominate the locality, as seen in this early postcard view of Hinton Road. (Lens of Sutton)

11.6   Loughborough Junction signal box was known as "The Tower" and was in use until 1981. This 1959 photograph shows C class no. 31480 runnng from the north to the east and passing the platforms disused since 1925. (P.Hay)

11.7   A Cricklewood - Sevenoaks class 319 unit was recorded on the same curve, while working a Thameslink service on 16th February 1990. It was photographed from the only platform remaining in use; those on the curve to Brixton had been closed in 1916. (J.Scrace)

12. BLACKFRIARS

12a. Background

The first Blackfriars station was the terminus of the LCDR's Metropolitan Extension and was on the south bank of the Thames. It opened in June 1864, but trains crossed the river from December of that year to a station north of the present one. The link enabling passengers to reach North London was completed in 1866, but the current station did not open until May 1886. It was named "St. Paul's" until 1937.

A second and wider bridge was built east of the original in 1886 and the first one was dismantled in 1984-85. The station was very extensively rebuilt in 1973-77 and most of its original features were lost, but the three terminal platforms were retained as was the roof above them.

12b. Services in 2002

The off-peak timetable offers eight Thameslink trains per hour, four running via London Bridge and the others through Elephant & Castle. At peak times, they almost all have to run via the latter station.

Connex use the terminal platforms for two Sevenoaks trains per hour, off peak. At peak times there are eight up and four down trains, two of which at each end of the day operate to and from City Thameslink, where there are two berthing sidings underground.

12c. Thameslink 2000 proposals

The fundamental alteration involves massive structural changes to transpose the through and terminal platforms and to reverse the use of the lines on the bridge.

The southward extension of platforms and their canopies most of the way across the bridge caused vociferous objections due to their serious intrusion into the London landscape, particularly when viewed from adjacent bridges. An amended design was produced, but many objectors remain. The platforms proposed were of such length as to occupy the entire bridge and thus to allow passenger access from the South Bank.

12d. RADIAL RAIL

No station or platform alterations are required, other than the lengthening of the two through platforms for 12-car trains. These extensions need have no visual impact if they are devoid of canopies. Most passengers are aware of which part of the train in which to travel in inclement weather, moreover few platforms are protected their full length elsewhere.

There would be no track transpositioning, as the pair on the east side of the bridge would be dedicated to CRT3 trams, as would the existing terminal platforms. As sidings would no longer be required, space could be made available for a footway on the east side of the railway bridge from which the vista would include the City, plus the elegant Millenium Bridge.

As at Charing Cross, there would be some loss of through travel opportunities (by those using Connex trains), but the list of direct destinations would increase greatly. This would be further supplemented by CRT3 trams linking many South London locations.

Some Connex train services could be extended to terminate at City Thameslink, depending on path availability until the core section reaches maximum capacity. Others would be terminated at the south end of the bridge at the proposed Tate Modern station, from where there would be opportunity to cross the river every 2-3 minutes by RR train or CRT3 tram. The proposal is explained in the next chapter in more detail.

12e. Route options

A	North - South East via London Bridge
B	North - South West via Waterloo
C	North - South Central via Cannon Street
D	North - South Central via Elephant & Castle

The route diagram is in paragraph 4.c.1 and the potential destinations are listed in chapter 16.

Reference: Pictures 28 to 39 in *Holborn Viaduct to Lewisham*.

12.1   The bracings of the original bridge can be seen on the left of this northward view, recorded in the 1950s. The nearest parts of the platforms are over the river. The next four photos are from that decade as well. (Lens of Sutton)

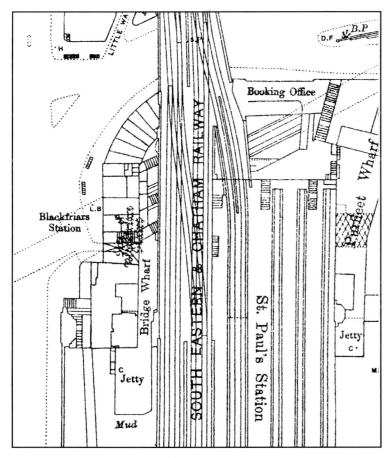

12.2   This plan of 1916 shows the three 1886 terminal tracks and the two through lines connecting with the earlier quadruple track, which was always devoid of platforms here.

12.3   The plan on the previous page shows platforms each side of each terminal track. This was altered prior to electrification in 1925 to the arrangement seen, which still applies now. (Lens of Sutton)

12.4   A view across the bridge from the up through platform (no. 5) includes the original Blackfriars station in the distance. This suffered greatly during the bombing raids in World War II. (Lens of Sutton)

12.5   The north facade was shrapnel scarred, but retained its stonework carved with potential destinations. Dirty and in shadow here, the stones were cleaned and incorporated in the new booking hall during a total rebuild in 1973-77. (Lens of Sutton)

12.6   All three terminal platforms contained trains of two 4EPB units on 13th April 1982. Articulated tramcars are much shorter and would not impede the view of St. Pauls Cathedral from Blackfriars Bridge when laying over here. (J.Scrace)

12.7 Looking north from platform 4 in October 1988 we see the 1974 bridge span over Queen Victoria Street and two Thameslink class 319 trains. Both sides of them are the white banded brick towers that once formed the southern corners of Ludgate Hill station. (A.C.Mott)

12.8 Stepping back three coach lengths, we witness the arrival of a Thameslink Luton - Purley stopping train in May 1989. Wider sliding doors are planned for replacements of the 319s, as congestion is intolerable in peak hours. (A.C.Mott)

12.9   Compare this picture with 12.7 and it is clear that Queen Victoria Street bridge has been inclined. The far end was dropped 1.26m in May 1990 to create a 1 in 29 gradient down to a new underground station (see 14.5). This and the following pictures are from November 2002. (V.Mitchell)

12.10   A Sutton-bound four-car class 319 waits at platform 4. No. 3 would not be required with the implementation of RADIAL RAIL and thus the tracks and platforms in the foreground could be slewed to the right to permit lengthening of the latter without extending the ugly structure which projects from the bridge to support the components on the left. (V.Mitchell)

12.11   *This is part of the treasured cityscape to be conserved and improved by the measures described. The twin towers of Cannon Street are left of centre and the white block is above the platforms. The bridge with only one support visible is the once-mobile Millenium Footbridge. (V.Mitchell)*

12.12   *A southward view of Blackfriars Junction has the lines to Metropolitan Junction curving to the left. A steel framework would be required to carry CRT3 trams over these.   No. 33114 is hauling the 13.33 "Premier Charter" from Blackfriars to Sevenoaks on 9th November 1991.   (B.Morrison)*

13. TATE MODERN (Proposed)

13a. Background

The LCDR opened its short-lived terminus on the South Bank on 1st June 1864 and it remained in use for passengers until 1885. The surrounding extensive goods depot functioned until 1964, after which time some sidings were retained for berthing peak hour trains, but part of the site was disposed of for office development.

The junction with the 1878 spur to the SER at Metropolitan Junction was (and still is) known as Blackfriars Junction.

13b. Benefits of a new station

i)   This area of Southwark has been subject to extensive office development in recent times, but has been remote from main line stations and would be enhanced by the proposal.

ii)   Many buildings are in residential use and the occupants would have the advantages of improved transport, notably the provision of light rail rapid transit.

iii)   The rush hour crowds presently having to walk across Blackfriars Bridge could join their trains or trams south of the river.

iv)   There would be excellent access from four routes (see 13d) to the developing leisure attractions of the area, notably the modern art gallery and the Globe Theatre.

v)   Blackfriars station would not require the expensive rebuilding envisaged in Thameslink 2000.

vi)   The treasured vista of the City from the west would be preserved.

13c. Features

i)   There are currently five parallel tracks, plus some vacant railway land, in this vicinity. This would allow space for platforms for both heavy and light rail services to be built.

ii)   Provision could be made for a bay platform for some of the trains presently terminating at Blackfriars, if these could not be incorporated in through RADIAL RAIL services.

iii) Space allows for a flyover to carry CRT3 trams over the curve to Metropolitan Junction. Its southern end would be on the bridge over the Charing Cross lines.

iv) Although within sight of Blackfriars station, the distance between it and the proposed station is 50% greater than that between Blackfriars and City Thameslink.

v) The entrance would be in Southwark Street, close to Blackfriars Road, where several train operating companies have their offices. They are at present curiously remote from a station.

13d. Route options

All routes from the North to the South East, South Central and South West lines chosen for RADIAL RAIL services, i.e. A to D, would serve Tate Modern. The route diagram is no. 4.4 and the potential destinations are listed in chapter 16.

Reference: Details of the past of this location can be found in pictures 40 to 44 in *Holborn Viaduct to Lewisham.*

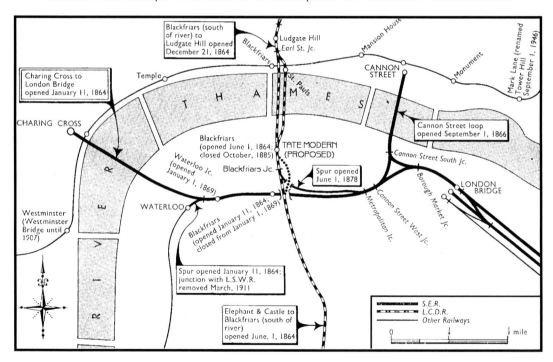

13.1   Diagram to show the pre-1899 ownerships. The dots indicate the position of the proposed single track flyover for the CRT3 tramway, which could have similar current collection to the Docklands Light Railway. The two might eventually be connected by a tunnel under Queen Victoria Street. (Railway Magazine)

14. NORTH OF BLACKFRIARS

14a. City Thameslink

The City terminus for trains from the south was Holborn Viaduct from 1874 until 26th January 1990. Its platforms were quickly removed soon after to enable a new and much lower station to be opened on 29th May 1990. It was called St. Pauls Thameslink.

In the preceding two weeks, the bridge over Ludgate Hill was removed and the tracks lowered under the street. The present name was used from 30th September 1991.

Provision was made for 12-car trains, although these are still awaited. Two berthing sidings (known as Smithfield Sidings) were laid, despite the spare track capacity northwards and vacant sidings in North London.

There had previously been four underground carriage sidings here. Two platforms for North-South trains were in use from 1874 until 1916. They were named Snow Hill until 1912 and Holborn Viaduct (Low Level) thereafter.

The elimination of termination at this location would be envisaged when the maximum of 24tph was provided.

Photos 6 to 27 in *Holborn Viaduct to Lewisham* give the background to the complex railway history of this area of the City.

14b. Farringdon

The Metropolitan Railway's Farringdon Street station opened in 1863 and the two parallel platforms for North - South services came into use in 1866. The station was "Farringdon & High Holborn" until the present title was adopted in 1936.

Following withdrawal of N-S trains in 1908, all trains from the south ran through to Moorgate, where they terminated until withdrawn in 1916. The introduction of Thameslink services in 1988 brought a new importance to the station as an interchange point.

The Thameslink 2000 proposals identified the need to improve the arrangements for passengers changing trains here, but six years have elapsed with no enhancements. This is despite many people changing between Thameslink and the Circle and Metropolitan Lines, including the routes to Amersham and Uxbridge. A new station building was also included in the scheme.

The station became the changeover point from AC overhead line to DC conductor rail. Operational difficulties with the pantographs have given rise to numerous delays here, with the consequent blockage of the entire system. Crew changes have also taken place here.

14c. Moorgate

The Metropolitan Railway reached here in 1865, "Moorgate Street" remaining a terminus until 1875. A separate but parallel terminus was built for trains from North London, it opening on 1st July 1866. By 2002, the terminal platforms were used in peak hours only, other than in emergencies.

The Thameslink 2000 plan envisages closure of this branch, despite protestations. The reason given is the need to extend Farringdon's platforms for twelve coaches.

The benefit of RADIAL RAIL is that an alternative City station would be available to many travellers, following the closure of Moorgate. This would be Cannon Street and up to 12tph would be routed to the City's southern district.

14d. King's Cross Thameslink

The present station in Pentonville Road is unsatisfactory, as it is remote from the main terminus and the associated Underground railway platforms. It is an even longer walk through busy streets to St. Pancras station.

The latter is being developed to become London's second international terminus and associated with this complex task is the provision of new 12-coach platforms underground for Thameslink trains, between King's Cross and St. Pancras stations. It is to be known (curiously) as St. Pancras Midland Road.

The work in hand also involves provision of connections between Thameslink tracks and the GN main lines north of the new station. These will enable through running to locations north-east of London.

14.1   On the right are the electrified tracks immediately north of Blackfriars platforms 4 and 5 and on the left are the non-electrified quadrupled tracks which served Ludgate Hill station, seen left of centre. The station had two island platforms when opened in 1865, but one was removed in about 1910. (Lens of Sutton)

14.2   Moving to the north end of the platform, we have the two electrified tracks curving right to the Holborn Viaduct terminus and those dipping under the signal box on the left are the tracks for steam-hauled freight trains between North and South London. (Lens of Sutton)

14.3   The remains of the platforms at Holborn Viaduct Low Level are evident in November 1953, as ex-Midland Railway 0-6-0T no. 47209 starts the steep climb to the signal box seen in 14.2. The station was opened as "Snow Hill" in 1874, renamed in 1912 and closed in 1916. (P.Hay)

14.4   A westward view down Ludgate Hill on 18th January 1990 features the 1866 bridge, which would be demolished a few weeks later. The entrance for the new station is under construction on the left. It would be called St. Pauls Thameslink, but only until 29th September 1991. It has been City Thameslink subsequently. (A.C.Mott)

14.5   *Looking north from the new down platform, we see the remains of part of the roof over Holborn Viaduct station concourse. The station closed on 26th January 1990 and the remaining three of its six platforms were quickly removed. (A.C.Mott)*

14.6   *A second photograph from 7th June 1990 shows the new station while it was open to daylight. The platform canopies are temporary, as the whole would soon be encased in a square concrete tube. (A.C.Mott)*

14.7 The LT Farringdon platforms are on the right of this picture taken in poor visibility in 1955. The goods yard is on the left, this closing in the following year. Steam trains ran in the peak hours to Moorgate on these lines and meat was conveyed from Acton to Smithfield over the single line connection. (V.Mitchell)

14.8 No. 319397 is Brighton-bound on 4th July 1999 as it passes over the site of the connection with LT at Farringdon. It will soon lower its pantograph and pass over the junction with the Moorgate line. The northern end of the conductor rail is in the foreground. (B.Morrison)

15. RELIABILITY

15a. Trains

As already mentioned the AC/DC changeover being at Farringdon can cause serious delays consequent to "technical problems". Thameslink 2000 envisaged transfer of this operation to Blackfriars.

RADIAL RAIL extends most changeover operations (and drivers) to Cannon Street, for a number of good reasons, to minimise delays:

i) Most important is that a train failing to changeover can remain in one of the seven platforms, while its passengers are transferred to the following train in an adjacent platform.

ii) The crippled train can be moved, using DC, into one of the two existing sidings.

iii) Triple track on West Curve would also give the opportunity for recessing and passing delayed trains.

iv) The stationing of a rescue locomotive ("Thunderbird") at Cannon Street would help to resolve problems with failed trains, notably those subject to flooding north of Farringdon. Such a centrally located power unit could potentially serve in an emergency all routes radiating from Waterloo, Elephant & Castle, London Bridge, St. Pancras and Kings Cross, plus the West London Line and lines north thereof.

v) Rolling stock flexibility would be improved by the use of push-pull fitted AC locomotives able to propel a DC EMUs northwards and return to the buffer stops at Cannon Street. Such traction units could wait there for another EMU to buffer up in times of stock shortage or other operational difficulties. Eleven coaches might be the maximum and axle loadings might restrict locomotive choice.

vi) Break of service between the two halves of Thameslink has caused unacceptable inconvenience to travellers, when northern trains terminate at Moorgate and southern ones at Blackfriars. Such regular harassment would end if most trains reverse at Cannon Street. The others could do so at Tate Modern, if necessary.

vii) When blockades are necessary between Blackfriars and Hendon, Brighton - Bedford services could be diverted via Waterloo, Barnes and Acton Central, given minor electrification extensions.

15b. Drivers

Driver availability is fundamental to train service reliability, but this obvious fact is not fully appreciated by some contemporary railway accountants, many of whom are unfortunately from other industries. The need to keep some drivers on standby or on call was recognised by operators in the past and numbers should now be reviewed, particularly with such complex operations as RADIAL RAIL.

Standby drivers could be profitably employed in many ways, notably learning other RADIAL RAIL routes with videos and simulators. For maximum availability, drivers would ideally sign for most or all of the routes of RADIAL RAIL.

The need for drivers to change ends would be minimised and limited to off-peak short trains. A driver would always be rostered to be ready to enter the rear of a reversing train to minimise dwell times.

15c. Track

Point failures can so often be remedied by the simple application of a crank handle. Prior to privatisation and the consequent division of responsibilities, such handles were kept locally and station staff trained in their use.

Subsequently, an engineer has had to be summoned, often from a remote location and subject to London's traffic congestion. A new strategy would be needed, particularly in the central area, where there are so many critical junctions.

It seems that track inspection routines have had common sense reapplied since the Hatfield disaster, but special attention visually and ultrasonically would be required at the heavily used junctions in the hub area.

Track circuit failures are a common cause of traffic interruption. Additional means of train detection should be implemented, in critical areas in particular. These would indicate on the signal panels with supplementary lights, but not control signal aspects. The techniques include axle counters, treadles (used for more than 100 years), optical detectors (beam interruption) and global positioning satellite technology (used by ScotRail).

CCTV would enable signallers to use their eyes again during track circuit failures and to keep the trains running safely. Such cameras would also help to reduce delays due to vandalism and trespass. They would be a small price to pay for increased reliability on these three accounts, particularly in the hub area.

Catch points with sand drags would be installed at all junctions. These safety devices were in wide use for more than a century, but have been greatly reduced in number. The recent disasters at Southall, Ladbroke Grove and Cowden could have been prevented or greatly reduced if catch points had diverted the erring driver.

However, many such points simply derail trains. If a sand drag is provided over a pair of rails parallel to the running rails, then the errant train is retarded and can be returned easily to its correct path, if speeds are low. They would be so in the hub area and normal service could be resumed quickly, with minimum injuries. Such a system would be of particular value on the many viaducts and is employed on one in Cornwall.

15d. Adhesion

Wheel grip for traction is considered here. Adhesion for retardation is included later. Your author has actively campaigned for adequate sanding equipment for many years, for both these reasons. While it has at last been made a requirement for all new stock, much of it is not totally effective and many old units continue to run with the equivalent of bald tyres.

With a 1 in 29 severe gradient for southbound trains up into Blackfriars, it is essential that good sanding is provided. However, excessive sand causes track circuit failure, hence the emphasis on this problem in section 15c. The tolerances are finely balanced, thus the need for "belt and braces" train detection in this critical location.

For reliability of the system, all routes would have to be completely cleared of lineside vegetation, which has grown up in the last 40 years of neglect. Many of the "leaves on the line" have been grown on railway land, but a start has been made to reduce these linear forests.

Wheel grip when braking is essential, but often lacking due to sand deficiency. Most of the unsafe trains are being phased out, but the new ones will have to be improved to provide a reliable and safe RADIAL SERVICE of full intensity.

15e. Bridge bashing

Occurrences of tall road vehicles hitting overbridges cause frequence disruption, often unnecessarily, as most incidents are of no consequence. RADIAL RAIL services would pass over a large number of bridges and modern communication systems have been identified for disruption reduction due to inappropriate closures.

16. DESTINATION OPTIONS

16a. Thameslink

The outer limits were, and still are, Bedford and Brighton, with Guildford and Sevenoaks being reached by secondary routes at different periods.

16b. Thameslink 2000

The proposal included extension to Peterborough and King's Lynn northwards and Littlehampton, Eastbourne and Ashford southwards. The French RER was linked with these ideas, but the relationship between population density and distance is very different in France.

16c. RADIAL RAIL

The policy of minimising distance for reliability reasons and maximising use of high traffic stations for service and revenue reasons would be employed. Thus, listed below are some of the places that would be considered for the radiating routes listed in paragraph 4.c.1.

A	Hitchin - Sevenoaks
B	Cambridge - Haslemere
C	Bedford - Brighton
D	Luton - Sutton
E	Watford Junction - Hayes
H	Windsor & Eton - Gillingham

Routes C and D are as at present.

Route E would run via Kensington Olympia and Waterloo and could be extended to St. Albans Abbey to make more use of this branch, but platform lengthening would be needed. Some trains could use the Silverlink DC lines, but a reversal near Willesden Junction High Level would be required.

Route H could be marketed as "Thameside" to tourists, as it would serve the castles at Windsor and Rochester, together with the maritime attractions at Greenwich and Chatham.

A Basingstoke to Colchester service operated from September 1999 until September 2002, but was too slow, as it had to use the congested North London Line. Such trains could use RADIAL RAIL, if provision was made for them to run on the Channel Tunnel Rail Link between St. Pancras and Stratford.

Ashford is not included in RADIAL RAIL, as it will have a greatly enhanced service to London in the near future, when the CTRL comes into use. Trains will connect with RADIAL RAIL at St. Pancras.

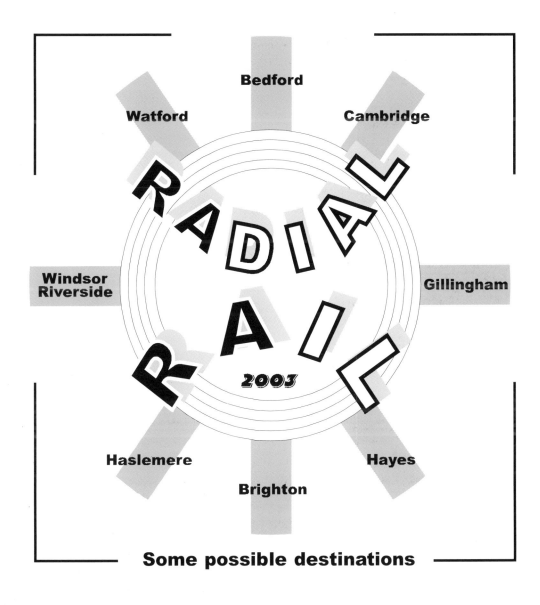

Bedford

Watford

Cambridge

Windsor Riverside

Gillingham

RADIAL RAIL

2003

Haslemere

Hayes

Brighton

Some possible destinations

17. CONCLUSIONS

17a. Objections to Thameslink 2000

i)   The destruction of the northern wing of the historic train shed at London Bridge station.

ii)   The imposition of an additional viaduct over Borough High Street and Borough Market, with consequent environmental and heritage issues in the Conservation Area.

iii)   The loss of the irreplaceable panorama of the City from the west by building a new station for Blackfriars above the river.

iv)   The cost benefit analysis results of the above are comparatively poor.

v)   The remote destinations and consequent delay potential would adversely affect reliability.

17b. RADIAL RAIL benefits

i)   **All the foregoing objections to Thameslink 2000 are overcome.**

ii)   Minimum alterations would be required at London Bridge and the train shed would be preserved . With up to six extra through trains per hour, fewer terminal platforms would be required. No. 8 would be removed to make way for a new no. 7 to serve the one through line presently devoid of a platform.

iii)   Destination choice for Southwark residents would be enlarged greatly.

iv)   City workers would have fewer changes, as direct travel opportunities would be increased substantially.

v)   The improved reliability features would impact significantly on all travellers.

vi)   The creation of RADIAL RAIL allows the construction of rapid transit routes to serve the West End and also the City, greatly enhancing travel from the South London areas devoid of Underground services.

vii)   The utilisation of the three cross river railway bridges would be improved by a large factor, reducing the loadings of the nearby road bridges.

viii)   There would be minimum planning requirements, as most alterations are on railway property.

ix)   Users of Channel Tunnel trains would have improved direct travel opportunities at both London termini.

x)   The Heritage Sites would not be impacted upon and the City panorama would be unspoilt.

17c. Implementation

RADIAL RAIL could be implemented in stages and funded accordingly.

Route C (Bedford - Brighton via Cannon Street) could be implemented at the next timetable change, subject to grade junction capacity considerations and signalling provisions being suitable. Four peak hour trains terminating at Cannon Street would become through trains, albeit of only eight coaches.

Blackfriars through platforms could be extended to take 12 cars by closing platform 3. Assessments show that platforms 1 and 2 could accommodate the terminating services by adjusting layover times. The need for 12-car trains is top priority and the work at Farringdon and King's Cross (St. Pancras) would need expediting as promptly as possible.

Detailed in-depth studies and model programmes for all junction occupancies would be required to establish capacities and to create indicative timetables provisionally.

Draft plans have been made for sequencing the alterations at Waterloo to avoid delays.

17d. The Way Forward

This raft of ideas for RADIAL RAIL is intended as a basis on which initiatives can be applied to ensure success for the benefit of travellers in London, a great city still awaiting integrated light and heavy rail modes of mobility.

A long-standing proposal (Crossrail) offers, long term, full size tunnels between Paddington and Liverpool Street, with extensions beyond, but at a massive price. The "Thameside" route (H) of RADIAL RAIL gives a parallel, albeit less central, route at a tiny fraction of the expenditure, but still linking outer suburbs with the City.

The way forward with the challenge herein is seen to be to focus on a commitment to serve London's travellers, to elevate them above mere customers, recognise them as passengers and to provide them SOON with an enhanced link serving, ideally, eight points of the compass, instead of two.

Launched in 1997, an amazing nine years after Thameslink itself, Thameslink 2000 is now stale and regarded by many as over ambitious and inconsiderate of Southwark and heritage alike. A 21st century approach to this 19th century problem is offered for urgent consideration.

RADIAL RAIL could become the flagship venture in the SRA's new projects portfolio and thus the premier jewel in its crown long term. Resource maximisation regarding land and rolling stock would minimise capital requirements for this high profile and beneficial strategy.

RADIAL RAIL journey times between newly connected places would be much better than previously and more places would be connected.

Fortunately, the climate for implementation and funding seems to be improving. The new Transport *for* London has initiated many commendable schemes and is actively promoting CROSS RIVER TRANSIT. Network Rail has largely superseded the much criticised Railtrack and has been declaring its intention to encourage initiative. The Strategic Rail Authority has been awaited by travellers for more than 150 years and has recently stated that "our approach to our work includes a sense of pride and a 'can do, will do' attitude".

FINSBURY PARK, KING'S CROSS, LONDON BRIDGE, and WOOLWICH.—G. N. & S. E. & C.

17.1   Bradshaw published this north-south timetable in January 1901. Note that it included some reversals at Cannon Street.

17.2   Part of the SECR timetable published by Bradshaw in July 1906.

UP.   **Week Days**—*Continued.*

18. LONDON BRIDGE SAVED

This section was not included in the RADIAL RAIL study, due to space limitations. It serves to further emphasise the importance of the proposal to minimise alteration of this station, whilst increasing its through capacity and making provision for Bedford - Brighton services in the peak hours.

18.1   The southern part of the station (left) was built as a terminus by the London, Brighton and South Coast Railway and is seen more clearly in the next photograph. The first terminus was opened by the London & Greenwich Railway in 1836 and was near the centre of this picture. The London & Croydon Railway's station was built to the right of it in 1839. The two exchanged stations in 1844 and the companies eventually became part of the South Eastern Railway. (Lens of Sutton)

18.2   The LBSCR train shed was photographed in 1882 with their wider than average coaches and their successful "Terrier" 0-6-0Ts in evidence. Their highly ornamented Terminus Hotel was built at the far end of the platforms. (Lens of Sutton)

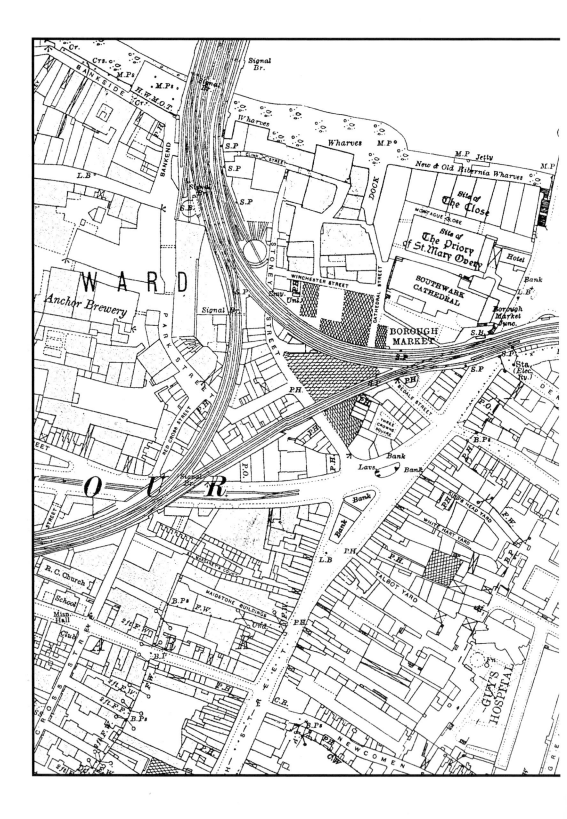

18.3   This map overlaps 10.5 and is also from 1916. The two parts of the station are clearly shown; there was no connection between them until a doorway was created in 1928. The widening of the double track above Borough Market is a contentious issue today and is being strongly opposed. RADIAL RAIL makes it unnecessary.

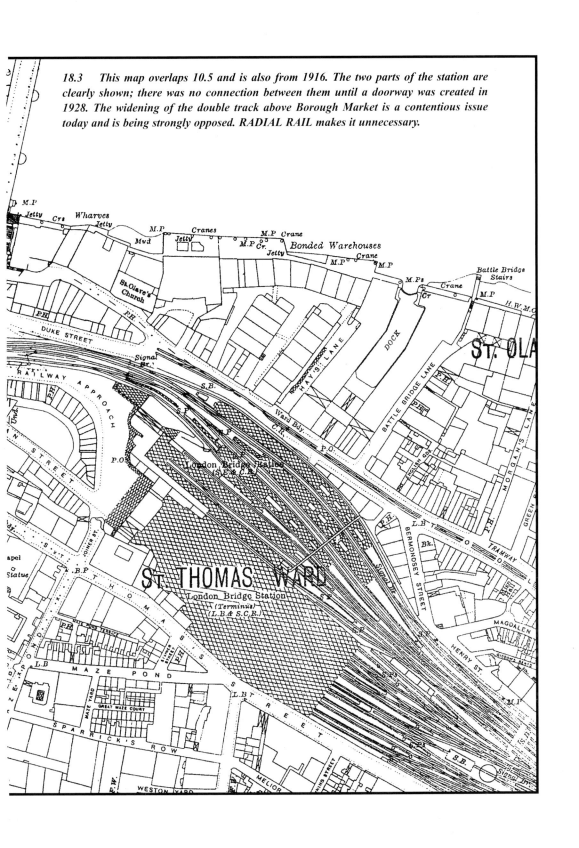

18.4   *Three photographs taken from the low level platforms on 12th September 1936 have features of interest. This shows the boundary wall (left) between the two formerly separate stations and a locomotive stabled in the short siding adjacent to it. No. 1592 was an ex-SECR 0-6-0 of class C.*
(H.F.Wheeller/R.S.Carpenter)

18.5   *No. 1227 is of the same class and is on another special train. Note that platform 9 has an engine release crossover, the only one at this station. Also evident are the two footbridges that linked platforms 1-10 and were erected in 1928. (H.F.Wheeller/R.S.Carpenter)*

18.6   The photographer turned round to record a not uncommon event. A locomotive has stalled on the sharp curve at the west end of platform 7, with its train standing on the 1 in 103 up gradient. "Schools" class no. 913 Christ's Hospital *is about to assist from the rear. (H.F.Wheeller/R.S.Carpenter)*

18.7   The Terminus Hotel and various station offices were destroyed by bombs in December 1940, leaving this gap. RADIAL RAIL would prevent an even greater loss on the other side of the structure.
(Lens of Sutton)

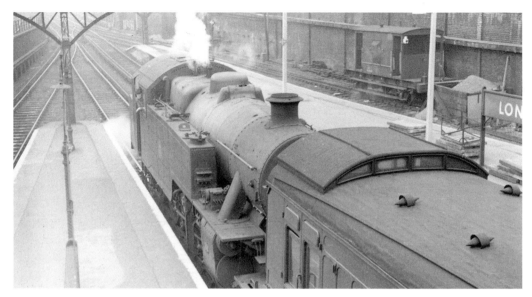

18.8   Platform 9 again and an opportunity to admire the "Birdcage" provided by the SECR for its guards to check that drivers had observed signals correctly. CCTV is now often provided inside trains; its extension externally would increase safety at minimal expense. The SR used periscopes. (V.Mitchell)

18.9   Entering platform 1 from Charing Cross on 10th July 1958 is "Schools" class no. 30924 Haileybury. The elevated hut housed the platform announcer. There was no platform 5 at this time, but there was a fifth track devoted to northbound goods trains. This part of the station had been rearranged in 1936-37. (H.F.Wheeller/R.S.Carpenter)

18.10 The all-Pullman "Brighton Belle" was a rare visitor to London Bridge, but was diverted here on 19th April 1969 due to engineering work on its usual route to Victoria. Its elegance is complemented by the splendid roof; it is the right part that is under threat of destruction, which would leave an asymmetrical structure. (E.Wilmshurst)

18.11 The ambience could be appreciated on a quiet day in April 1976. The 1928 signal box (centre) had recently been superseded by the panel box on the right of the tracks. The platforms were renumbered at this time. The old nos 20-22 had been lost in 1972. (J.Scrace)

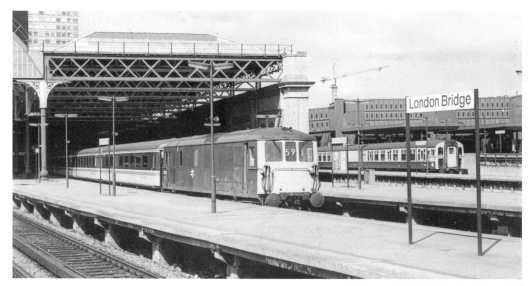

18.12   Electro-diesel no. 73103 was working a special on 2nd April 1984 to Haywards Heath using the stock of a Gatwick Express, a rare sight here. If the branch to Heathrow Airport from Feltham is built, then *RADIAL RAIL* could offer a direct service between the airports which is required by many international passengers. Running via Cannon Street, they could be offered views of St. Pauls and Tower Bridge at no extra charge. (J.Scrace)

18.13   The alterations of 1975-78 resulted in Cannon Street services using platforms 1 to 3 exclusively and Borough Market Junction being eliminated. The up passenger loop (under the left signal) came into use for non-stop trains in April 1976. Work is in hand in July 1991 to prepare for the repositioning of platforms 4 to 6 in July/August 1993. No. 7 was closed, leaving no. 8 as the only low level platform outside the main roof. (V.Mitchell)

18.14   A train leaves platform 6 on 9th November 2002, formed of class 465 stock on a North Kent service. RADIAL RAIL would require reduction of the building in the distance (which was used by Royal Mail until their traffic was rerouted) and provision of a platform on the site of the concrete wall. New connections would be needed at the far end of the platforms. The traveller's environment could be improved by using daylight on the bridge featured and its congestion would be reduced as RADIAL RAIL would reduce the amount of train changing here. (V.Mitchell)

This and most of the other stations under consideration are featured in the *SECR Centenary Album* and *South Eastern & Chatham Railways*, the complete history of the system. All are listed on the next page, together with *London, Chatham & Dover Railway*.

The significance of RA RA on the title page of this publication is to represent the RA signal given to drivers and seen at the end of many platforms. It indicates Right Away, which means "time to move" or "get going" and is used here as a hint to all concerned to do just that. London's passengers have been waiting for more than five years for Thameslink 2000 - World War II was fought and won in that period, without undue dithering. They deserve better. Readers who have comments on the proposals herein can send them to:

Strategic Rail Authority
London Integration Team
55 Victoria Street
London SW1H 0EU

Transport *for* London
Rail Services Team
42-50 Victoria Street
London SW15 0TL

Middleton Press

Easebourne Lane, Midhurst, W Sussex. GU29 9AZ Tel: 01730 813169 Fax: 01730 812601
Email: enquiries@middletonpress.fsnet.co.uk   *If books are not available from your local transport stockist, order direct with cheque, Visa or Mastercard, post free UK.*

BRANCH LINES
Branch Line to Allhallows
Branch Line to Alton
Branch Lines around Ascot
Branch Lines to Ashburton
Branch Lines around Bodmin
Branch Line to Bude
Branch Lines around Canterbury
Branch Lines around Chard & Yeovil
Branch Line to Cheddar
Branch Lines around Cromer
Branch Lines to East Grinstead
Branch Lines of East London
Branch Lines to Effingham Junction
Branch Lines around Exmouth
Branch Lines to Falmouth, Helston & St. Ives
Branch Line to Fairford
Branch Lines to Gosport
Branch Line to Hayling
Branch Lines to Henley, Windsor & Marlow
Branch Line to Hawkhurst
Branch Lines around Huntingdon
Branch Line to Ilfracombe
Branch Line to Kingsbridge
Branch Line to Kingswear
Branch Line to Lambourn
Branch Lines to Launceston & Princetown
Branch Lines to Longmoor
Branch Line to Looe
Branch Line to Lyme Regis
Branch Lines around Midhurst
Branch Line to Minehead
Branch Line to Moretonhampstead
Branch Lines to Newport (IOW)
Branch Lines to Newquay
Branch Lines around North Woolwich
Branch Line to Padstow
Branch Lines around Plymouth
Branch Lines to Seaton and Sidmouth
Branch Lines around Sheerness
Branch Line to Shrewsbury
Branch Line to Swanage *updated*
Branch Line to Tenterden
Branch Lines around Tiverton
Branch Lines to Torrington
Branch Line to Upwell
Branch Lines of West London
Branch Lines around Weymouth
Branch Lines around Wimborne
Branch Lines around Wisbech

NARROW GAUGE
Branch Line to Lynton
Branch Lines around Portmadoc 1923-46
Branch Lines around Porthmadog 1954-94
Branch Line to Southwold
Douglas to Port Erin
Douglas to Peel
Kent Narrow Gauge
Northern France Narrow Gauge
Romneyrail
Southern France Narrow Gauge
Sussex Narrow Gauge
Surrey Narrow Gauge
Swiss Narrow Gauge
Two-Foot Gauge Survivors
Vivarais Narrow Gauge

SOUTH COAST RAILWAYS
Ashford to Dover

Bournemouth to Weymouth
Brighton to Worthing
Eastbourne to Hastings
Hastings to Ashford
Portsmouth to Southampton
Ryde to Ventnor
Southampton to Bournemouth

SOUTHERN MAIN LINES
Basingstoke to Salisbury
Bromley South to Rochester
Crawley to Littlehampton
Dartford to Sittingbourne
East Croydon to Three Bridges
Epsom to Horsham
Exeter to Barnstaple
Exeter to Tavistock
Faversham to Dover
London Bridge to East Croydon
Orpington to Tonbridge
Tonbridge to Hastings
Salisbury to Yeovil
Sittingbourne to Ramsgate
Swanley to Ashford
Tavistock to Plymouth
Three Bridges to Brighton
Victoria to Bromley South
Victoria to East Croydon
Waterloo to Windsor
Waterloo to Woking
Woking to Portsmouth
Woking to Southampton
Yeovil to Exeter

EASTERN MAIN LINES
Barking to Southend
Ely to Kings Lynn
Ely to Norwich
Fenchurch Street to Barking
Ilford to Shenfield
Ipswich to Saxmundham
Liverpool Street to Ilford
Saxmundham to Yarmouth
Tilbury Loop

WESTERN MAIN LINES
Didcot to Banbury
Didcot to Swindon
Ealing to Slough
Exeter to Newton Abbot
Newton Abbot to Plymouth
Newbury to Westbury
Paddington to Ealing
Paddington to Princes Risborough
Plymouth to St. Austell
Princes Risborough to Banbury
Reading to Didcot
Slough to Newbury
St. Austell to Penzance
Swindon to Bristol
Taunton to Exeter
Westbury to Taunton

MIDLAND MAIN LINES
Euston to Harrow & Wealdstone
St. Pancras to St. Albans

COUNTRY RAILWAY ROUTES
Abergavenny to Merthyr
Andover to Southampton
Bath to Evercreech Junction
Bath Green Park to Bristol
Burnham to Evercreech Junction
Cheltenham to Andover
Croydon to East Grinstead
Didcot to Winchester
East Kent Light Railway
Fareham to Salisbury
Guildford to Redhill
Reading to Basingstoke
Reading to Guildford
Redhill to Ashford
Salisbury to Westbury
Stratford upon Avon to Cheltenham
Strood to Paddock Wood
Taunton to Barnstaple
Wenford Bridge to Fowey
Westbury to Bath
Woking to Alton
Yeovil to Dorchester

GREAT RAILWAY ERAS
Ashford from Steam to Eurostar
Clapham Junction 50 years of change
Festiniog in the Fifties
Festiniog in the Sixties
Festiniog 50 years of enterprise
Isle of Wight Lines 50 years of change
Railways to Victory 1944-46
Return to Blaenau 1970-82
SECR Centenary album
Talyllyn 50 years of change
Yeovil 50 years of change

LONDON SUBURBAN RAILWAYS
Caterham and Tattenham Corner
Charing Cross to Dartford
Clapham Jn. to Beckenham Jn.
Crystal Palace (HL) & Catford Loop
East London Line
Finsbury Park to Alexandra Palace
Holbourn Viaduct to Lewisham
Kingston and Hounslow Loops
Lewisham to Dartford
Lines around Wimbledon
Liverpool Street to Chingford
London Bridge to Addiscombe
Mitcham Junction Lines
North London Line
South London Line
West Croydon to Epsom
West London Line
Willesden Junction to Richmond
Wimbledon to Beckenham
Wimbledon to Epsom

STEAMING THROUGH
Steaming through Cornwall
Steaming through the Isle of Wight
Steaming through Kent
Steaming through West Hants

TRAMWAY CLASSICS
Aldgate & Stepney Tramways
Barnet & Finchley Tramways
Bath Tramways
Brighton's Tramways
Bristol's Tramways
Burton & Ashby Tramways
Camberwell & W.Norwood Tramways
Clapham & Streatham Tramways
Croydon's Tramways
Dover's Tramways
East Ham & West Ham Tramways
Edgware and Willesden Tramways
Eltham & Woolwich Tramways
Embankment & Waterloo Tramway
Enfield & Wood Green Tramways
Exeter & Taunton Tramways
Greenwich & Dartford Tramways
Hammersmith & Hounslow Tramwa
Hampstead & Highgate Tramways
Hastings Tramways
Holborn & Finsbury Tramways
Ilford & Barking Tramways
Kingston & Wimbledon Tramways
Lewisham & Catford Tramways
Liverpool Tramways 1. Eastern Routes
Liverpool Tramways 2. Southern Rout
Liverpool Tramways 3. Northern Route
Maidstone & Chatham Tramways
Margate to Ramsgate
North Kent Tramways
Norwich Tramways
Reading Tramways
Seaton & Eastbourne Tramways
Shepherds Bush & Uxbridge Tramw
Southend-on-sea Tramways
Southwark & Deptford Tramways
Stamford Hill Tramways
Twickenham & Kingston Tramway
Victoria & Lambeth Tramways
Waltham Cross & Edmonton Tramw
Walthamstow & Leyton Tramways
Wandsworth & Battersea Tramway

TROLLEYBUS CLASSICS
Croydon Trolleybuses
Derby Trolleybuses
Hastings Trolleybuses
Huddersfield Trolleybuses
Maidstone Trolleybuses
Portsmouth Trolleybuses
Woolwich & Dartford Trolleybuses

WATERWAY ALBUMS
Kent and East Sussex Waterways
London to Portsmouth Waterway
West Sussex Waterways

MILITARY BOOKS
Battle over Portsmouth
Battle over Sussex 1940
Bombers over Sussex 1943-45
Bognor at War
Military Defence of West Sussex
Military Signals from the South Coas
Secret Sussex Resistance
Surrey Home Guard

OTHER RAILWAY BOOKS
Index to all Middleton Press statio
Industrial Railways of the South-E
South Eastern & Chatham Railway
London Chatham & Dover Railway
London Termini - Past and Propos
War on the Line (SR 1939-45)

BIOGRAPHY
Garraway Father & Son